THE SUMMER KING

H. Holtein Pinxit   W. bolbet Sculp

THEODORE ANTONIO
Baron NEUHOF
First King of Corsica.

THE MONARCH MIDDLE-AGED
From an Engraving in the British Museum

THE SUMMER KING

*Variations by an Adventurer on
an Eighteenth-century Air*

AYLMER VALLANCE

THAMES AND HUDSON
LONDON

Contents

Contents

Illustrations

By Way of Introduction

LAPPED by the warm Ligurian Sea, a bare hundred miles south of Nice and half that distance from the coast of Italy, lies the mountainous island where Napoleon Bonaparte was born. Dying in St Helena, he said that he had but to close his eyes for the remembered scent of Corsica to fill his nostrils. It was in a high Corsican village, the still air laden with the smell of sun-drenched *maquis*, that I conceived the idea of writing this story of a man whose renown no Pantheon perpetuates, but who cut a dramatic figure— bizarre, knavish, romantic, as you please—in the island's fortunes, two centuries ago.

For lovers of the romance which clings to lonely moors and mountains, our own age of populous tourism exacts its price—in Corsica as in the Scottish Highlands. When James Boswell, Esq., visited Corsica in 1765, he observed ruefully that, outside the French and Genoese garrison towns, he found but one solitary inn, which lacked sadly the comforts of London's coffee-houses. Today, the coaches which bring the cameras of Birmingham and Detroit to Glenfinnan are matched by the French Line ships and Air France planes which land throngs of holiday-makers at Ajaccio. There, in the shops which sell souvenirs on the Cours Napoléon, they happily buy, as keepsakes, little badges enamelled into the Arms of Corsica—the Moor's head and the links of broken chain. Few inquire what is the origin, or the meaning, of that emblem; and, if they were asked what incident it commemorates, most of the shopkeepers would be puzzled to find an answer.

Contemporary Corsica is proud of Napoleon, prouder still, perhaps, of its heroic son, Pasquale Paoli, who fought so stubbornly for independence in Bonaparte's despite. But most Corsicans have forgotten, or (it may be) purposefully put out of mind, the earlier episode in their long struggle for freedom which gave them, for one long summer, two centuries ago, an elected king. Yet it is to him that they owe their Arms: he posed as the liberator who broke the islanders' chains; and he arrived, fantastically, from Barbary. Those of them who know the story have (I think) an uneasy feeling that the gallant record of their eighteenth-century resistance is not enhanced by the partisans' acceptance as legitimate monarch (no matter how brief the reign) of a personage to whose record cling the tattered rags of so many dubious adventures.

King Theodore I—the first and last occupant of a throne in Corsica—died and was buried, just two hundred years ago, in Soho. Whatever Corsicans may feel, the bi-centenary of his death in England seemed to me to be occasion for dredging, with an exploratory bucket, the silt of eighteenth-century material—documented fact, less reliable gossip and pure myth—which has settled on this nearly forgotten adventurer's career. The picture of the man, to be intelligible, needs its frame, its historical setting; and that I have tried to provide. I make no claim to have added important fresh knowledge for the serious historian. Indeed, lack of precisely verifiable facts, which Lytton Strachey cheerfully declared to be the "first requisite" for the writing of successful history, is a factor with which an honest biographer of King Theodore has to deal. In the "reconstruction" attempted in the pages that follow, I have tried to follow faithfully the extant documentary evidence; but probability, as discern-ing readers will detect, has on occasion had to do service in certainty's stead.

What brooks no question is the indomitable spirit of the Corsicans who chose, however ill-advisedly, to elect Theo-dore as their lawful king. They had their faults—as had the adherents of that other, more glamorous Pretender who un-folded in 1745 his standard at Glenfinnan—but, from 1729 onwards, they fought toughly for their wild, almost impassable mountains against alien oppression. They held life cheap; they could be cruel, some were little better than bandits; their loyalties were always bedevilled by jealousies, clan feuds and vendettas. But they had the saving virtue of the courage which never gives in. To that virtue the crumbling towers on the Corsican coast—sole relics of Genoa's past domination—stand even today as monuments.

As for the other personages who make their appearance on this eighteenth-century stage, virtue is hard to find. Of the "great" men under whose shadow King Theodore played his part—Görtz, Alberoni, Ripperdà, Francis of Loraine and Victor Amadeus of Savoy—Alberoni alone had, perhaps, integrity; and even of that one cannot be too sure. To the rest one may fairly apply Robert Burns' phrase, "Sic a parcel o' rogues"—and chief rogue of all was Theodore I himself: this is a book without a hero. Not even the English come well out of it; indeed Corsica owes little gratitude to "perfidious Albion". When they occupied the island in 1794-6, ostensibly backing Paoli, but in reality exploiting the Resistance against the arch-foe Napoleon, the English (let us be frank) were only repeating the tactics which they employed—less effectively—when a British warship carried ex-King Theodore to Corsica, fifty years earlier.

That dust has settled: English visitors to Corsica today need fear no vendetta for ancient national wrongs. As fancy takes them, they may tan their skins on the beaches of the west coast, which King Theodore never saw, but whose eucalyptus-fringed *golfes* are busy today with the camps of Eclaireurs de France; or they may follow perspiring parties of Catholic schoolgirls (roped to sternly celibate young curés) up the hot rocks of Monte Cinto. If they are so minded, they may visit Aleria, on the east coast, where our story begins. There are oysters to be had from the nearby Etang de Diana; but otherwise little of note. Aleria was never a favourite town of the Corsicans, and there is an old saying: "*Aleria, Aleria, chi non ammazza vituperia*" (she curses those she does not kill). Even today there are mosquitoes. So on, then, before the sun sets, to Bonifacio and its succulent lobsters. If you seek Theodore's grave, it is within a stone's throw of Piccadilly Circus that you will find it—not in the island where he wore a crown.

The duty of the biographer, it has been said, is not to preach, nor to defend, but to "expose". If this is not an edifying book for young persons, the fault lies in the times with which it deals. The epoch of George II and Louis XV was an ebullient, but not an edifying period: credulity and villainy, craft and folly, jostled each other on the stage. My concern has been simply to lift one little corner of the long-fallen curtain.

Corsica, 1954—London, 1955   A. V.

March Morning at Aleria

IT was March 12, 1736, and—on the east coast of Corsica —a fine morning: the south-west breeze carried down to the small seaport of Aleria the heady scent of myrtle, lentisk and cystus from the mountains inland. Save for a few fishing smacks, the harbour was empty; but watchers on the shore, as the sun drank the last of the sea-mist, glimpsed a sail on the southern horizon. Standing on her course, her canvas all set, the ship came up rapidly. She was a small brigantine, registered in Plymouth and under British colours; she had come from North Africa. Outside the little port, she hove to, fired a salvo of cannon which brought no answer, and dropped anchor.

She had evidently been expected; for a rowing-boat promptly left the shore, manned by two fishermen, their brown backs bent to the clumsy oars. In the stern were four Corsicans—men clearly of some standing—scarlet waist-bands under their jackets of black velvet cord, long muskets slung over their shoulders. On and off, since 1729, the Corsicans had been in revolt against Genoese oppression, and the insurgents, three weeks ago, had captured Aleria, with four brass cannon (so the *London Daily Post* sympathe-tically reported) as "well-earned" booty. These then were rebel patriots, led by one Xaviero di Matra, who were rowed out to the brigantine. The boat drew neatly alongside; a rope-ladder was let down; the Corsicans, encumbered by their muskets, clambered up. The ship's master, an undis-tinguished Englishman who had become involved in a strange and hazardous ploy, greeted the rebel leaders politely and escorted them to the poop, where the passengers whom the Corsicans had come to meet were waiting in a carefully staged group.

The leading personage, whom the patriots addressed respectfully as "Excellency", was a remarkable figure. Superb on the deck, he wore a scarlet Oriental caftan, down to his heels, and was shod in bright yellow Moorish slippers; his full-length, well-curled and powdered perruque was crowned by a Cavalier hat, the brim turned up at one side; from his waist hung a long Toledo sword; and in one hand he carried an Indian cane with a beak-shaped crook. Behind him, bare-headed, stood his retinue, nearly a score of attendants—as would become a man of high rank. There were two French officers and eleven Italians, who included a swarthy aide-de-camp, Christoforo Buongiorno, a sleek chaplain, a secretary, a young soldier called Bigani, a Lord High Steward, a household steward, a cook and uniformed lackeys. There were also a Turk called Monte Christo, three Moorish slaves and two Corsicans, Quilico Fascian-nello of Aleria and Patrone Francesco of Cap Corse, whose freedom from slavery in Tunis the "personage" had recently[1] purchased—not, however, for cash but on credit!

Details of the financial terms on which this transaction in ransom had been concluded were naturally not disclosed by "His Excellency"; and his ostensibly generous, compas-sionate act was warmly applauded by Xaviero and his friends. They were still more favourably impressed when

Buongiorno, attentive to a lordly wave of the "personage's" hand, produced the ship's manifest and read out the list of the cargo—cannon, muskets, sacks of grain and leather Arab shoes, to say nothing of casks of bullion in the shape of Barbary gold and Tunisian *zecchini*.

Long parleys followed in the stateroom below the poop; and the rowing-boat was sent back to the shore carrying an urgent letter, of which more later. "His Excellency" desired to be fully informed of the attitude of all the rebel chiefs. "Was it true that many of them had been talking of surrender, of giving up the struggle? And how formidable and aggressive were the Genoese garrisons?" Fired by the thought of all those arms and coins—why, the very pockets of the retinue jingled as they moved—the Corsicans were bold and confident. "The Genoese were craven dogs who did not dare to stir from their fortifications. Now that these supplies, praise God, had arrived, the tyrants would be driven into the sea within a month." To back these assurances, the breeze carried from the (now crowded) shore the sound of cheering: the news brought by the rowing-boat had spread.

It soon spread far beyond the walls of Aleria. Reports of this landing, on a troubled island which many powers were then jealously watching, were soon to sweep through every European capital. Rumour had wings. The "unknown" who had brought this succour to the rebels and was offering himself—would you believe it?—as their king, was a man of high estate; he was Charles Edward Stuart (then sixteen and safely in Rome); he was Francis Rakoczy, the ex-Prince of Transylvania (who was, in fact, dead); he was the Comte de Bonneval, that fiery-tempered French soldier of fortune who joined the Turkish Army and became Osman Pasha; he was Baron Ripperdà, the fallen Chief Minister of Spain, making a come-back from his exile in

Tetuan; he was the Duke of Ormond or some other leading Jacobite. Embassies and newspapers vied with each
other in efforts to learn the identity of the man—and, still
more important, of his backers—who had reached Corsica
with regal ambitions, and proposed to wrest from the
Republic of Genoa this strategically important, if turbulent,
colony.

In the previous year, a General Assembly of the Corsican
insurgents had passed a resolution "that the Virgin Mary
be the protectress of Corsica". It was not, however, any
divine personage who landed in March 1736, nor was it
even the terrestrial prince of any empire—least of all, Charles
Stuart. It was a nimble-witted, plausible, attractive and
quite unscrupulous German adventurer—Baron Theodore
Stephan von Neuhoff. At forty-two, after a career spent in
"secret service", political conspiracies and still less reputable
private chicanery, he was making a bid—no less—for a
throne. It is with his chequered fortunes that this book will
deal.

It will be, as I have said, a book without a hero. Neuhoff
had his defenders,[2] both during his life and after his death
in London, just two hundred years ago. Prince von
Grimberg, who commanded a regiment of Bavarian
Guards in which Theodore once served, wrote[3] in 1776
that his young lieutenant had been "a man of warm temper,
brave enough, and had a good share of wit". Another contemporary, the Comte d'Apremont, describes him in his
youth as "tall, well built, witty, very attractive—a man to
whom nothing seemed difficult". Charm indeed he had:
that and quick wits were the stock-in-trade which carried
him—until his final, sorry decrepitude—through fifty years
of gambling, cheating, borrowing, dubious intrigues and
bare-faced roguery. Warm temper one may deduce from
the portrait reproduced as frontispiece to this book; and

there is evidence of it in some episodes to which we shall
come. But of real bravery I can present little evidence. Those
wary, wide-open, calculating eyes were those of a Bayard in
reverse—a *chevalier d'industrie* neither *sans reproches* nor without fear. If, like many men in that age of sanguine gamblers,
he discounted difficulties, his confidence was rooted in
vanity, his courage (such as it was) in arrogance.

Neuhoff's career, both before and after the bizarre episode
in Corsica, became a legend from which an honest
biographer has to discard many accretions of falsehood.
Chevrier,[4] who went to the island during 1740, "searching
for the truth", found that most of "Theodore's admirers",
whom he interrogated, were "either liars or ill-informed".
Parts of the myths attached to his life are due to Genoese
"psychological warfare". Seeking to discredit Neuhoff,
Genoese broadsheets ascribed to him, at the time when he
landed at Aleria, "a pig's paunch, a prematurely grizzled
beard when he was not shaved, and an ugly mouth from
which two upper teeth are missing"—a description belied
by later portraits "from life". Darkness, in some phases of
Theodore's career, is made darker by the fact that, as secret
agent, he was at pains to cover his tracks, and that he was
at nearly all times a monumental liar.

Fortunately, he was a prolific writer of letters. They,
combined with the accounts of his contemporaries, from
Corsican patriots to Horace Walpole, give us the picture
of a "gentleman-crook" who lived by his wits in a corrupt
and cynical age. Disgraced and stripped of his army commission at an early age, taught by his subsequent employers
the arts of espionage and "underground" diplomacy, he had
few scruples left in his moral luggage when he came to
Corsica. Pretending always to noble aims and "obligations
of honour", this German baron, who stood, arrayed
fantastically like Solomon, on the brigantine's poop, was,

from first to last, a rogue with a nimble tongue. Self-indulgent, his acts of seeming generosity were never without calculation; and he was always ready to betray, without compunction, those who trusted him. Prodigal with promises which he could not fulfil, and to which he never intended to be loyal, he was proposing, in 1736, to turn a brave people's revolt against tyranny into a sordid commercial speculation for his own ends, and to make a market in monarchical honours. For this soldier of fortune, this play-actor, with all an actor's vanity, whom the English ship had brought to Aleria that morning, had arrived in Corsica with no sincere attachment to the insurgents' cause. Having spent much of his life on the fringes of the profitless movement to put the Stuarts back on the throne of England, he was now concerned—with less idealistic motives than those of the Jacobites—to win, in Corsica, a crown which could be turned to commercially profitable account.

What distinguishes Neuhoff from the common run of adventurers and confidence tricksters is that he did actually become a king—though his reign was brief. He was, wrote Boswell later, "a most singular man" who might, with better luck, have achieved his aim. But he had been "so beaten about, by change of fortune, that he had lost the common sentiments of mankind, and viewed things as one who is mad, or drunk, or in a fever. He had nothing to lose and a great deal to win." The verdict is charitable. The man who became a legitimate monarch, and wore a crown through one hot Corsican summer, had something in him, no doubt, of the eighteenth-century gambler's fever (his were the days, remember, of the South Sea Bubble and John Law's famous System); but, though he had certainly little to lose, he was not a madman but a clever rogue who succeeded, by sheer effrontery, in focusing, for a short spell, the limelight of European power-politics on his doings. All that one can say in his favour is that he wore his roguery, like the fancy dress in which he landed at Aleria, with a *panache*: he cut a figure in the world. But if he had less luck than James Boswell would have wished for him, he got in the end no more than his deserts. In this posturing play-actor's final scene—when the footlights were dimmed, the costume threadbare—there may, if you like, be room for pity. Even so, sympathy shrugs a slightly contemptuous shoulder. *Pace* Boswell, Neuhoff was never entitled to blame fortune: he was his own executioner.

CHAPTER ONE

Spring-time of an Adventurer

BORN in Cologne, on August 24, 1694, Theodore von Neuhoff came[5] of a family of proud and impoverished gentry, who lived near Ludenscheid, in the county of Marck, in Westphalia. His grandfather[6] had "grown grey in arms", commanding a regiment for that truculent prelate Bishop Bernard von Gallen. His father, Anton, was first sent to study at Liége; there was talk[7] of his entering the Church. The grizzled colonel, however, insisted that only the profession of arms would become a von Neuhoff. So Anton accepted[8] a commission in the bodyguard of the Bishop of Münster. Even in that generation, however, there seems to have been a touch of irregularity in the make-up of the von Neuhoffs. Anton, forgetful of Ludenscheid's tradition of correctness, contracted a *mésalliance* which out-raged his family: he married Amelia, the daughter of a draper in the small town of Viseu, near Liége. (One class-conscious chronicler[9] has it that the lady was of better social standing—the daughter of an "inspector of fortifications"; but this unacceptable account goes on gaily to relate how Anton fell gloriously at the siege of Namur in 1792, two years before Theodore's birth!) The draper (for such he was) inconsiderately died within a year of his gaining this

8

titled son-in-law, and left his daughter the disappointingly small sum of 11,000 florins. On the income from this modest marital heritage, coupled with the pay attaching to the command, which he managed to obtain, of a modest fort near Metz, Baron Anton and his wife—exiled to French service through the wrath of the family in Westphalia—had to live.

Two children were born of the marriage—Elizabeth and Theodore Stephan. Baron Anton died prematurely in 1695, at the age of thirty-four. Widowed, Amelia in due course re-married; her second husband was a Customs official at Metz, by name Marneau. During her widow-hood she had retired from Metz to a quiet village in Lor-raine. But was she entirely alone in her grief? Not so, if we are to believe the British agent (see Appendix II) who supplied Mr Tilson, of the British Foreign Service at Han-over, with a *Letter from Paris*, which was duly passed, in June 1736, to the Embassy at Vienna, and now figures in the Robinson Papers in the British Museum. The Paris agent's story is that the Comte de Mortagne, equerry to "Madame", the Duchess of Orleans, was "*éperdument amoureux*" of Anton's widow; he not merely became Amelia's "protector" for a time, but took charge of the children. There is other evidence[10] to indicate that the count played an important part in the children's early life; but the guilty *liaison* between Mortagne and Amelia may well have been invented by the Genoese as part of their general "smear" campaign against the "vagabond of no fortune" who had landed in their island. At any rate, M Marneau was not deterred by current scandal from marrying a widow with two children.

Apart from Mortagne, Theodore and his sister had a kindly guardian in a (much older) cousin, Baron von Drost, a member, and later Grand Commander, of the

Teutonic Knights in Cologne. He placed Theodore at school with the Jesuits in Münster, and subsequently lodged him with a tutor in Cologne. There Theodore, according to a story with which he would often regale his boon companions in later days, had his first adventure. For this sober tutor to young sparks from Westphalia had two pretty daughters, with one of whom, by name Mariana, Theodore fell in love. All went well until the arrival on the scene of another young student, a wealthy count, who proceeded so steal Mariana's affections. The sequel, which Theodore would complacently relate, is in the best romantic tradition. It is Mariana's birthday: Neuhoff has a quarrel with his rival: there is sword-play in the professor's garden: the count falls dead. *Ben trovato*, shall we say? In reality, Theodore characteristically "improved" the facts and turned an angry bout of jealous schoolboys' fisticuffs into a fatal duel. In the eighteenth century, Casanovas were full-fledged at any early age, but Neuhoff was evidently romancing in his anecdotage. For by fifteen—too young surely for him to have killed his man!—he had become, through Mortagne's influence, page to "Madame", the Duchess of Orleans.

> My thanks for the [German] gazettes. They entertain me greatly; and when I have read them, I give them to two German Pages I have—a Neuhoff and a Keversberg.

So "Madame" wrote to the Raugrave Louise on July 23, 1709. She liked, and was amused by, her "graceful rogue", and took his sister also for a time into her household. According to a highly unreliable and flattering biography written in 1768 by a Polish adventurer[11] who posed as Theodore's son, the young page had early martial enthusiasms aroused by incessant study of Plutarch's *Lives*, which he read and re-read until he had them by heart. Here again we catch an echo of Neuhoff's later anecdotes about himself: in the riotous company of the Versailles *Corps des Pages* Theodore had merrier games to play than learning Plutarch by rote.

Mr Tilson's Paris agent was probably not far off the mark, nor even being malicious when he wrote that Theodore "showed himself adept in learning all that becomes a man of quality". (The attributes of such a man in the early eighteenth century had their defects.) As he grew up, the *Letter from Paris* continues, he became well built and good-looking: "*son air était noble*". But though he had "charm" (*douceur*) rather than "brilliance", his character was over-laid by inordinate vanity: "that—and debauchery—were his besetting sins". Certainly Versailles was no school for saints. While "Liselotte" spent her days either in full Court dress or in riding clothes, her pages—when not required to hang on her stirrup in the hunt—were free to gamble, fight the "town boys", and generally raise hell. And in the entourage of the ageing Roi Soleil and the household of "Monsieur", Duc d'Orléans, the estranged husband of "Madame", there were easy means for a personable young Westphalian to find a way of growing-up between scented sheets.

From the *Corps des Pages*—with or without real "martial enthusiasm"—it would be a natural step for a young German baron to obtain a lieutenancy in some regiment; and this step, according to a 1743 pamphlet[7] published in London, Theodore took when he was "big enough to deserve the name of a young man"—let us say, in 1711 or 1712, when he would be seventeen or, at most,[12] eighteen. His first commission[13] was in the Régiment d'Alsace; but this appointment was not to the young officer's liking. Garrison duty in Strasbourg meant the severance of many enjoyable amorous ties in Paris. So, with the aid of his young friend, the Marquis de Courcillon—Theodore had soon learned the value of useful friends in influential places—he transferred to the Régiment de Courcillon for a couple of years' easy soldiering, with plenty of Paris leave. This was a carefree period for Theodore (who had discovered how to "touch" a rich friend's purse), ended by young Courcillon's untimely death in 1714. After that, since Paris *congés* could no longer be financed out of a penniless lieutenant's pay, there was nothing for it but to ask "Liselotte" for a helping hand. The duchess, wagging a stern finger at Theodore for his extravagance and scandalously numerous "affairs", wrote none the less a commendatory letter to her brother, the Elector of Bavaria, and packed the young rascal, with his "nimble tongue", off to Munich.

There, in the Guards commanded by Prince von Grimberg, Theodore made a brave show—as would become a nobly born, not to say arrogant, young West/phalian baron. But his pay was miserably insufficient for the ostentation which he felt the world owed him. The gaming tables were the obvious solution. Stakes were high in Munich, the Guards officers were rich. Fortune smiled for a time, then frowned. In the summer of 1715, after a ruinous night of losses which could not be met, came disgrace. With the vanity of the crook who thinks he cannot be caught out, Theodore gambled with more than money—and lost.

According to the *Letter from Paris*, Theodore—without the purse of his friend Courcillon to help matters—was unable to pay his debts of honour, was sent back to Paris by the Prince von Grimberg, was *cité* ("carpeted") before the Marshals of France, and, failing to meet his obligations, was stripped of his commission and obliged to leave the country. "Madame", however, who was in a position to know the facts, has a more circumstantial, still less creditable, story of roguery to tell. In a letter which she wrote on October 20,

1720, "Liselotte" records that, to meet his gambling losses, Theodore borrowed money from two Knights of Malta, to whom he gave (in a sealed envelope) "advices" for repay- ment of the debt in Paris. These "advices" were addressed to his "uncle", M de Wendt, and his "aunt", Mme de Ratsamhausen. Both these personages were, in fact, members of the Duchess's household, but neither of them bore any kinship to Neuhoff; and when the sealed envelope was opened in front of the expectant creditors, it was found to contain blank sheets of paper: Theodore had written in vanishing ink. The scandal was great: "Liselotte" was a strait-laced (albeit coarse-tongued) old lady; and her brother Max-Emilian, the Elector, apprised of this *rouerie*, sent Neuhoff packing. Without money or honour, the disgraced young baron returned to Paris, where his sister had lately married the Comte de Trévoux.

"Madame" was very angry with Neuhoff; and in her letter, written five years later, she goes on to say that, back in Paris in 1715–16, Theodore "tried to kill his brother-in- law", then fled abroad with all the Trévoux cash he could lay his hands on. As Neuhoff stayed in the Trévoux *hôtel* on at least two later occasions, it is questionable whether the murderous attack on the count in 1715 could really have occurred. (One does not usually give renewed hospitality to a guest who has "tried to kill" one.) What Theodore undoubtedly did was to borrow all he could from his sister and her husband. With the proceeds of their (perhaps reluctant) generosity, he made his way to The Hague—then a centre of diplomatic intrigue. Dressed and lodged as became a "gentleman of condition", he made contact with Baron Görtz of Holstein-Gottorp, that faithful, ingenious and unscrupulous adherent to the disastrous cause of Charles XII of Sweden. The older man saw in the glib, good-look- ing young adventurer an *apprenti* "confidential agent" whose training might pay dividends. Theodore was "engaged" as a retainer; and for the next five years, from 1716 to 1720, his talents for secret diplomacy were harnessed to various unsuccessful plots and schemes to put the Stuarts back on the throne of England.

CHAPTER TWO

The Plotters' Man

THE spring of 1716 was not, it might be thought, a propitious moment for a penniless, disgraced, but still ambitious and extravagant soldier of fortune to attach himself, even at second hand, to the Jacobite cause. On February 21, "James III", the Old Pretender, had disembarked at Gravelines after a futile expedition to Scotland, which he was destined never to see again. Six months earlier, Louis XIV, whose domination of Europe had depended on friendship with a Catholic England, had died; and the Duke of Orléans, the new Regent, had little use for the fallen Stuarts and a keen sense of the value of friendly relations with England. Moreover, in 1713, the Treaties of Utrecht had paved the way for the easy progress of George Lewis of Hanover to the English throne on the death, in August 1714, of Anne, the last "legitimate" Stuart to wear the English crown.

As he rode, on a hired horse, to take wine at Baron Görtz's lodging in the Vijverberg, Neuhoff asked himself what the baron's invitation—following a meeting in the Spanish Embassy—might portend. There had been brief talk, guarded but intriguing, of "benefits" in connection with the "king over the water". Neuhoff had no ideological devotion to the Jacobite interests for which, it had been suggested, he might work. The question he asked himself, cursing the melting snow which splashed him from the horse's hoofs, was how Baron Görtz could imagine at this date that Stuart chestnuts could be pulled from the fire, or at least that poor James Francis Edward could have, for the enemies of England, a nuisance value.

Before the log fire, a flagon of sack on the low table between him and his guest, Görtz was adroitly talkative: a generation's history came smoothly, succinctly, from his lips. True enough, the Grand Alliance which Dutch William had formed with Austria, Holland, Denmark and Savoy, had challenged and curbed the hegemony of France in Europe: Tyrconnel's rising in Ireland, with French backing, had ended disastrously in the Battle of the Boyne; and, in Scotland, Claverhouse had paid with his life for the brittle victory of Killiecrankie. But that, said Görtz, was an old story now.

Neuhoff, stretching his snow-splashed legs towards the blazing logs, listened without enthusiasm. Viscount Dundee was dead before he was born; the Peace of Ryswyk, with William III recognized by Louis as the legitimate King of England, had been signed while he was in his cradle. What was all this history to him? His thoughts wandered. If only he had "made" that girl in the Elector's Court before the cursedly unlucky night at cards.

Görtz poured another glass of wine, coughed softly and resumed. Things, he admitted, had gone well for Hano-verian England. It had been a mistake on Louis XIV's part to accept the crown of Spain for his grandson Philip, Duc d'Anjou, and to recognize "James III", on his father's death in 1701, as King of England. The Emperor, claimant to the Spanish throne on the Archduke Charles's behalf, had been affronted and thrown (politically), with Savoy, into the arms of that stupid Queen Anne; Marlborough and his fiery ally, Eugène of Savoy, had broken Vendôme's armies at Ramillies and Malplaquet; "James III's" expedi/ tion from Dunkirk to Scotland in 1708 had been ignomi/ niously dispersed by Admiral Byng in the North Sea; and though England, wearied of the long war, had turned out the bellicose Whigs, dismissed Marlborough, and patched up a Tory treaty with France at Utrecht, the Stuart cause had gained little from it all.

"Is that so?" Neuhoff yawned behind his hand. The wine was good, his manners admirable. But where, in the name of all the petticoats in Paris, was this leading?

No, said Görtz; Bolingbroke had been a man on whom reliance could not be placed—a trembling reed. Pro/Stuart, he had fled from England when Anne died and George Lewis of Hanover took up the succession with a new Whig parliament to back him. Joining "James III" at Bar/le/Duc as Secretary of State, he had disapproved, last August, of Mar's foolishly precipitate rising at Braemar, but had not had the power of decision to prevent James's futile sally to Peterhead and back.

"Doubtless," said Neuhoff, his mind turning to the little matter of an unpaid bill for lodgings. Where, in all this, did an ex/officer of the Bavarian Guards come in?

Görtz reached the point. Eighteen months ago, his royal master, Charles XII of Sweden, had returned from his long exile in Turkey—aftermath of a crazily venturous invasion of Russia, which cost him at Poltawa the flower of Sweden's forces—only to find that George I of England (hitherto inclined to favour Sweden as a counterpoise to Russia) had evolved a greedy scheme for a partition of the Swedish possessions: Denmark would get Schleswig/Holstein; Hanover, Bremen and Varden. Hard pressed by hostile Danes, Poles and Russians, Charles had escaped, that

winter, from the ruins of Stralsund, and was now threatened
with an invasion of Sweden. Could not a relieving diversion perhaps be organized in his interests?

After all, said Görtz, the Treaties of Utrecht had left
some untidy ends. Philip of Spain had had to cede Sicily
to that greedy upstart, Victor Amadeus of Savoy: he was
still smarting at the loss. James III, forced by the Regent to
leave Lorraine, was still at Avignon; the Highlands were
embittered; the Continent was cluttered with pro-Stuart
exiles; and there were still Jacobites in England. A descent,
or at least the threat of a descent, on Scotland by the Swedish
forces now in Christiania might be feasible—might it not?
—if Stuart adherents in England put up some money?

Half asleep till now, Neuhoff sat up with a jerk: his
boots shook the slumbering logs into new flame. Money?
The word was magic. If diplomacy might mean money, he
would be a diplomat with a will. Rising, he bowed to
Baron Görtz. "I am yours to command," he said; "what
are your instructions?"

They were prompt in coming: Neuhoff was to act as
courier between Baron Sparre, the Swedish Minister in
Paris, and Count Gyllenborg, the Swedish Ambassador
in London. Sparre, said Görtz, was in touch with "James
III" at Avignon, while Gyllenborg had already induced
the English Jacobites to subscribe £30,000. This money
had been remitted to Görtz at The Hague, and used by
him in purchasing six vessels for the Swedish navy:
indeed it is evident that Görtz was as cynically disinterested
as Neuhoff was in the merits of the cause of the fallen
Stuarts. His real concern with the embers of revolt still
smouldering after "the Fifteen" was to raise Jacobite funds
which could be discreetly diverted to his own (hard-
pressed) royal master's cause.

This exercise in political "high finance" appealed strongly

to Theodore: it looked much more profitable and—with
powerful protection—much safer than trickery at the
expense of tiresome Knights of Malta who made a ridiculous
fuss about a few *livres* and demanded their money back.
He was quick to see that the English Jacobites must be
induced, by word from Paris and The Hague, to believe
that strong foreign support for the luckless James Edward
could, after all, be mobilized. Görtz's little "briefing" in
the past twenty years of Europe's diplomatic history con-
vinced Theodore that his own talents would have been
wasted had he stayed on in those dull Bavarian Guards.
His lost commission, revoked by the Marshals of France?
Tush! He was still Baron von Neuhoff, Freiherr of
this and that, a handsome German gentleman of "condition". His purse filled by Görtz's secretary, Theodore
cheerfully took up his duties as confidential postman and
agent de liaison.

Paris was too unhealthy to visit openly: the tricked
Knights of Malta were threatening pains and penalties, and
there were other debts, contracted in the gay times of service
with young Courcillon and still unsettled. One or two
stealthy trips from The Hague to Sparre's Embassy were
made by Neuhoff in disguise; but the dispatches from
Paris, whose encouraging tenor (it was hoped) would
loose faithful Jacobites' purse-strings across the Channel,
were generally brought to The Hague by another of Görtz's
agents. London, however, was safe: the authorities there
had nothing yet against Neuhoff.

During the summer and autumn of 1716, Görtz's personable young emissary could often be seen strolling innocently
around St James's—his pocket filled with that conspiratorial
correspondence which was subsequently published by the
British Government as evidence of the "Gyllenborg Plot".
There was time, too, for other diversions. Two pretty

ladies of easy virtue—so Theodore later was fond of relating complacently—vied with each other in teaching English to the young baron; and London tradesmen were obliging with credit to a fashionable foreigner evidently on close terms with his Ambassador. All in all, the apprentice king-maker had a pleasant time in London during his repeated visits in 1716.

It was too good to last. Back in The Hague, shortly before Christmas, Neuhoff found Görtz in a sour temper. Charles XII had firmly declined to put his name to any commitment involving an expedition from Norway to Scotland, and English subscriptions to the "Gyllenborg Fund" had lately begun to flag. Something must be done to rouse Jacobite enthusiasm. Could Theodore think of anything?

He could. He had a brilliant idea which showed that he had already become an apt pupil in the art of underground diplomacy. Hanoverian England, he said, was worried about the attitude of its ally, Russia. Tsar Peter was known to be sceptical of George I's professions of friendship, and rendered increasingly suspicious of his allies by the Danes' reluctance to begin the invasion of Sweden last summer. Suppose the English Jacobites could be shown a letter from Peter, hinting that, in return for the permanent cession of Mecklenburg (which his troops, to George I's rage, had recently occupied), he might support the Jacobites.

"The Tsar will never write such a letter," objected Görtz.

"Your secretary is a skilled penman," said Neuhoff.

So it was arranged. Peter's signature was easy to copy passably; the compromising letter was taken (as a potent aid to further money-raising) to Gyllenborg by Neuhoff, who landed from a Dutch smack near Gravesend, at the end of January 1717, shortly after the conclusion of the Triple

Alliance between England, Holland and France. Alas! Hurrying through the foggy evening to St James's, he learned that Stanhope, apprised of the Görtz intrigue, had just had the Swedish Ambassador arrested, and his papers impounded. For Neuhoff this particular game was up: no more agreeable lessons in English. Beating a hasty retreat to Gravesend and the waiting smack, he rejoined Görtz at The Hague. There Görtz himself was arrested and kept, until August, in prison by the States General at England's instance, while Theodore, who had seen to it that he was custodian of enough incriminating docu⁄ments to ensure powerful protection, found asylum in the Spanish Embassy.

There, for some weeks, he remained, discreetly removed from the States General's attention, winning a little at cards from the *attachés* and improving his Spanish. This was to be a useful addition to his stock⁄in⁄trade of talents. Görtz's confinement was by no means rigorous: through visitors from the Spanish Embassy he kept in touch with Neuhoff; and towards the end of March, Görtz's secretary came to see Theodore, bearing a well⁄filled purse and a letter of urgent instructions. To relieve the increasing hostile pressure on Sweden, something might yet be done by a Jacobite diversion organized, this time, with Spanish help. Neuhoff was to go post⁄haste to Madrid with letters for Cardinal Alberoni.

That adventurous cleric—son of a poor gardener in Piccuza—had made his way to Spain as Abbé attached to the train of the Duke of Vendôme in the War of the Spanish Succession; and, after Utrecht, had been appointed Parmesan Envoy to Philip V. In that strange, starchy, priest⁄ridden court, where the uxorious king obtained in bed all the pleasures he needed to complete days spent in interminable shooting and hunting, the business of State

was conducted largely by the young Queen—Maria Louise
of Savoy—and her indomitable Camerera Mayor, Madame
des Ursins, Louis XIV's unofficial legate to Madrid.
Alberoni watched and waited—acquiring popularity with
the Grandees by the famous *cuisine* of his table. Opportunity came to him in January 1714, when Maria Louise
died. Philip, unmoved by his wife's death (he went shooting on the day of her funeral), desired a successor in bed
who should be "docile". Alberoni suggested, and won
approval for, Elizabeth Farnese of Parma—a young lady
who compensated, in fact, for lack of looks by a con-
spicuous temper.

Met by Alberoni at Pamplona on her entry into Spain,
in December 1714, Elizabeth (at Alberoni's prompting)
picked a quarrel with Madame des Ursins and sent her
shivering over the Pyrenees into France. Philip, in bed, she
satisfied (he had a one-track mind) and enslaved. From
then on, though he was still officially the Parmesan Envoy
and no more, Alberoni was all-powerful in the Queen's
counsels. His primary aim was to secure for Elizabeth the
succession to Parma and Piacenza and, if possible (through
her Medici lineage), to Tuscany. But if the power of Austria
in Italy was to be permanently curtailed—and this was a
necessity in these plans—France and England must be
friendly, or at least neutral. With the Regent Orléans,
Alberoni kept on good terms; and England, he hoped,
had been "bought off" by the commercial agreement—improving for English slave-traders the Utrecht Treaty terms
—which he had negotiated with Methuen in December
1715.

Friendship, however, between Hanoverian England and
Papist Spain was not so easily to be secured. News of
Alberoni's activities in Spain since Elizabeth Farnese's
arrival alarmed George I and his advisers. Was the man

not reforming the army, promoting industries, rehabilitating agriculture, building ships, improving roads? In May 1716 George I reacted sharply: he made a new defensive alliance (the Treaty of Westminster) with the Emperor, Charles VI —an alliance which implied English support for the Emperor's cherished plan to acquire Sicily (ceded by Spain to Savoy at Utrecht) and to compensate Victor Amadeus of Savoy with the barren island of Sardinia. Alberoni and Elizabeth were furious; and when, in the early months of 1717, the aggressive Triple Alliance between England, Holland and France was signed, Alberoni finally decided that friendship with "treacherous" Hanoverian England paid no dividends. He got in touch with "James III", who had just then retreated from Avignon to Rome, and he wrote to Görtz inquiring whether Charles XII would be inclined to co-operate in a Jacobite move against England.

It was to that letter which Neuhoff carried Görtz's (quite fallaciously) optimistic answer; and his mission was to persuade the Cardinal that, if he acted "decisively", Stuart supporters would help energetically to disrupt the Triple Alliance's membership. Reaching Madrid in April 1717, Neuhoff found a diplomatic climate much to his taste, a climate propitious for mischief—against both the Emperor and George I. Alberoni, it is true, had wanted more time to strengthen Spain before making a move in the Mediterranean ("I need five years", he is reported as saying in 1715) but his hand was forced. A bare month after Neuhoff's arrival, the venerable Don José Molinès, travelling from Rome to Spain to take up the post of Grand Inquisitor, was seized by Prince Löwenstein, Austrian Governor of Lombardy, and clapped with contumely into prison. The devout Philip, outraged by this insult to the Church, clamoured for retaliation. Alberoni, a month later, dispatched an expedition which invaded and easily captured Sardinia—a convenient stepping-stone on the road to Tuscany. Spain was now definitely ranged against the Emperor, and hence, at one remove, against George I.

Posting back with this good news to Baron Görtz—now on the verge of release from incarceration at The Hague—Neuhoff did not fail to credit himself with having played a great part in swinging Spain into the anti-Hanoverian camp. He had been well lodged in Madrid, had cut a dash at Court as Charles XII's "confidential emissary", and had learned that nothing becomes a penniless adventurer so well as a cloak of "success" worn confidently with *bravura*. "The Cardinal," he said to Görtz, "trusts me as deeply as he loves the Queen." We may doubt the depth of Alberoni's confi-dence; but Görtz was sufficiently impressed to promise his agent ample money to carry on the good work in Madrid.

So, leaving Görtz—on his release in August 1717—to rejoin Charles XII, Neuhoff went once more to the con-genial atmosphere of Philip's Court. As go-between, he paid several further visits to Görtz, now at Gottorp, during the winter of 1717–18. The cardinal was eager for a definite Spanish-Swedish alliance against England, France and Austria, and Neuhoff, who had learned that promises cost nothing, assured him that he (Theodore) was the man to arrange it. "Görtz", he boasted, "is in my pocket." It may be doubted if the cardinal believed him, but he clearly had uses for this engaging rogue whom Görtz had sent him; and, from Neuhoff's point of view, Alberoni had one great advantage over the Swedish Minister: he had all the money in the world, and was liberal with it. A confidential talk with Görtz's secretary at Gottorp in April 1718 con-vinced Theodore that the position of Sweden was precarious: from then onwards, though he drew Görtz's pay, he became, more and more, the cardinal's man.

There was plenty of intrigue for an adroit agent in Spain during 1718; it was a year of undeclared wars and cynical power politics which finally persuaded Neuhoff that scruples were a liability in the quest for fortune. In July a Spanish expedition landed at Palermo, whose inhabitants welcomed the invaders: Spaniards began rapidly to overrun the island. With Austria now enrolled with England, France and Holland in a Quadruple Alliance— it was signed on August 2—Stanhope journeyed to Madrid. During his stay (its motive seems to have been to lull Alberoni's suspicions of England's intentions), Admiral Byng was ordered—though England was not at war with Spain—to seek and destroy the Spanish fleet in Sicilian waters. This he did, off Cape Passaro, on August 11. The attack, which the Spaniards regarded with some justice as a treacherous and piratical act, increased Alberoni's determination to disrupt the Quadruple Alliance—to which Victor Amadeus of Savoy now decided to adhere: it was his one chance of recovering Sicily or, in exchange, Sardinia. Neuhoff was now given a fresh task.

Sent for by the cardinal one evening in September, Theodore was told to go to Paris. He was to report to the Spanish Ambassador, Prince Cellamare, and, through him, to contact the Duchess of Maine, most active of the malcontents opposed to the personal rule of the Regent. Neuhoff went, borrowed money from the Duchess, and busied himself with the plot in hand. It was, however, a futile conspiracy, aimed at the Regent's assassination; it was speedily discovered by the Government's spies, with the result that the conspirators were arrested. Cellamare, with Neuhoff in his train, was sent packing as a requital for his complicity in the plot; and the British declaration of war on Spain (December 1718) was followed promptly by France.

That was not the sum of Alberoni's troubles, and Neuhoff himself had to cope with a reverse of fortune. During
the autumn, the Atlantic ports of Spain had been noisy
with the bustling assembly of an armada. Theodore, back
from his intrigue with Cellamare, kept up the pretence that
Görtz, at his instigation, would soon recruit Russia as ally
in the anti-Hanoverian campaign, and that Charles XII
was spoiling for revenge on George I. Meanwhile the
Court at Madrid had been filling up with Jacobite exiles.
With plans on foot for a Spanish expedition directed on
Cornwall, while the Swedes fell upon the east coast of
Scotland, the hopes of the Old Pretender in Rome may
well have revived. Alas! The death of Charles XII at
Frederiksten, on December 11, followed by Görtz's sum-
mary execution, shattered illusions based on a two-pronged
invasion of Britain from south and north. A sad disappointment for Alberoni, and a worse blow personally for Neuhoff: there would be no more money now from Gottorp,
and life on the grand scale in Madrid was not cheap. The
cardinal had been generous, spasmodically, but the baron
had no regular appointment, no Spanish stipend on which
he could rely. As he paced his garden one evening—
wondering if he had succeeded in making himself sufficiently useful to Alberoni, if the cardinal had forgiven the
Cellamare fiasco—that cutting wind of Madrid, which can
kill a man if it blows strongly enough to snuff a candle,
caught Neuhoff in the lung. For a whole month, fevered
and sick, he lay abed.

Fortune, however, was to smile again for this adaptable
chevalier d'industrie. As he lay sleepless in his room one night
in late January 1719, a dim figure softly crept through the
door: the moonlight through the window made visible
the livery of the cardinal's household. Tiptoeing towards the
bed, the visitor laid down beside it a heavy purse of gold:

Neuhoff was still in favour. And more was to come. Convalescent in February, Theodore was sent for by the cardinal and told that great things were afoot, despite the wreck of Swedish plans. "James III" had arrived from Rome and was regally installed in the Palace of Buen Retiro, together with the Duke of Ormond. Theodore was to help in the planning, after all, of an expedition against Cornwall, and was to accompany it as Alberoni's personal emissary. Meanwhile he should have the rank of colonel and a salary of 600 *pistoles*.

Ordering a uniform of appropriate magnificence, Neuhoff spent busy days hurrying between Madrid and Cadiz, where the armada was being prepared. He conferred self-importantly with Ormond, ingratiated himself with James Edward, clanked his new sword up many a conspiratorial staircase. He was now, in his own estimation, a king-maker—if only the Jacobites played the game.

The fate of that ill-starred expedition is history. The fleet —five warships and twenty-two transports—sailed from Cadiz early in March. It was to pick up Ormond at Corunna; but on the passage the convoy met severe weather off Cape Finisterre and was disastrously dispersed. A subsidiary expedition directed against Scotland—two frigates with 300 Spanish infantry, arms and money— sailed, with Earl Marischal, from Pasages; and the earl's brother, Keith, left from Le Havre, in company with Seaforth and Tullibardine, in a small vessel. On March 30 the two parties of Jacobites met at Stornoway; and though counsels were divided—Tullibardine was reluctant to act until they had firm news of Ormond's arrival in England —the little force landed in Kintail on April 14, and endeavoured to raise the clans.

The response was half-hearted—as well might be in face of Ormond's fiasco; and in early June, Tullibardine, with

1,100 men, was decisively routed in the Pass of Glenshiel
by a Hanoverian force of inferior numbers which moved
against him from Fort Augustus.

> The hardy Marshal, I protest,
> He ran as fast as did the best.
> Lord Seaforth, that great Man of Mars,
> Was glad, like Mars, to show his arse.

That contemptuous doggerel of the day was the epitaph on
the ignominious failure of Alberoni's plans for a restoration:
the Jacobite cause was to be dormant for over twenty years.

Neuhoff, made cautious by the Cellamare fiasco and
having no mind to brave the discomforts of the Atlantic at
the spring equinox, had been at pains not to sail from
Cadiz. Waiting with Ormond at Corunna for the
armada's arrival, he made a fine semblance of eagerness to
fight for "the Cause", but was careful to cough heavily in
the duke's presence. "My lung, your Grace; still trouble-
some, I fear." Ormond was sympathetic. Since the fleet
never arrived, the play-acting could soon be abandoned.
Back in Madrid, his cough cured, Neuhoff found a more
congenial role than seafaring. He installed himself in the
cardinal's ante-chamber and "obliged" people who sought
favours or swift audience.

According to Mr Tilson's Paris agent, he became, in this
position, "vain and arrogant"—which seems likely enough
—and the same source credits him with having made,
through perquisites, a lot of money ("between 10,000 and
12,000 *pistoles*", i.e. £4,000–£5,000 sterling). Here one
suspects, in the light of later events, a considerable exaggeration. Neuhoff spent money prodigally; but, even on the
lights o' love who could be readily found in Madrid, he
could hardly have exhausted such large earnings so quickly
that, by summer, we find him going hat in hand to the

cardinal for an advance of pay, and even borrowing from moneylenders.

Alberoni, who had heard tales of his protégé's extravagance and loose living, gave Theodore a sober piece of advice. He had better settle down, take a wife with good connections. Always ready to adapt himself, Neuhoff looked around. His eye fell casually on Mary Sarsfield, one of the Queen's ladies-in-waiting. She was the daughter of an Irish Jacobite, Lord Kilmallock, and distantly related to Ormond. Did love enter into the affair? One concludes that it did not. By all accounts, Mary Sarsfield was ill-favoured, vain and graceless, *d'un humeur revêche*, according to Mr Tilson's *Letter from Paris*; worse still, this "sour-tempered" Irish girl had no talent for running a ménage in the manner demanded by a husband whose tastes had been formed in the luxury of Versailles. There were money troubles: Ormond—to Neuhoff's disappointment—did nothing to help; and, even with income from "ante-chamber" bribes, the salary from Alberoni was little enough for a married colonel with extravagant tastes. The marriage was unhappy from the start.

The sky was darkened, too, for Neuhoff, by the clouds gathering round his patron, Alberoni. With the bulk of the Spanish Army locked up in Sicily, French forces invaded Catalonia and the north-west of Spain; the arsenals at Vigo and Ferrol were demolished by raiding English ships; efforts to provoke a Breton rising against the Regent were abortive; and Philip V was beginning to long desperately for peace. Neuhoff began to wonder, in those early months of his marriage, if the time was not soon coming when he must seek yet a new employer. Loyalty was an ingredient missing from Theodore's character. Deciding that Alberoni would have to be "written off", he proceeded to cultivate acquaintance with Baron Ripperdà.

That wealthy Dutchman (he had married an heiress at
an early age) had been sent to Madrid as envoy of the States
General in 1715. He found the city congenial—indeed he
claimed to have Castilian blood in his veins—and in 1718
he quitted the Dutch service, turned Catholic, and (now a
luxurious widower) settled at Philip V's Court as a private
individual. With a Dutchman's commercial instincts, he
became manager of a cloth factory at Guadalajara, in which
the Queen was interested; and he had begun, by 1719, to
plan an influential part in the politics of Philip's Court. To
him Neuhoff offered his services as *homme de confiance*. The
offer was accepted. Ripperdà was never particular in his
choice of agents; and who knew but that this young baron,
with his training under Görtz, might not be of use? What
did Neuhoff want to do?

"I should like," said Theodore, "to raise a troop of Westphalian cavalry for service in Spain. But for that I shall
need money."

"Doubtless," said the Dutchman, smiling cynically, and
promised the cash. His purse was deep.

Neuhoff had correctly detected the way the wind was
blowing in Madrid. That autumn the Earl of Peterborough,
acting on the British Government's behalf, had visited
Parma and persuaded its worried Duke to write to Philip V
that there could be "no peace until Alberoni had gone".
The strategy worked: on December 15, Philip dismissed
and banished his adventurous and ill-starred adviser.
Cardinal Alberoni took ship for Italy, and found refuge
temporarily at Sestri di Levante. There, shaded by the
pines on the lovely little promontory, he could watch the
coloured fishing-boats—less perilous for the peace of
Europe than his armadas—drawn high, as they are today,
on the sandy beach.

Ripperdà was now soon to become the great power in

Madrid, but Neuhoff found it inexpedient, after all, to wait for his new employer's aggrandizement. An awkward circumstance stood in the way. Alarmed by Alberoni's decline, Theodore's many creditors had clamoured for prompt payment. There was one source only from which the most pressing claims could be satisfied—the money given by Ripperdà for the equipment of that "troop of Westphalian cavalry". Misappropriation? Neuhoff had no objections to that—after all, what else had Görtz done with Jacobite funds? But Ripperdà would demand an account, ing, and was a dangerous man to cheat. So, just before Christmas, on the morrow of Alberoni's going, Neuhoff packed his luggage, telling Ripperdà that he was off to Westphalia—for recruits. Taking advantage of the fact that Mary, his wife, was in attendance on the Queen at the Escurial, he rode hard to Cartagena and embarked for France. In his bags he had his wife's jewellery; and she, poor girl, was pregnant at the time. She died, according to the *Mercure de Hollande* (April 1740), in Paris, four years later, by which time her errant husband was far from France and otherwise employed; and the child of the marriage, a daughter, did not survive infancy. The exit of the "plotters' man" from confidential employment was not, one may say, exactly creditable.

CHAPTER THREE

Odyssey of a Free-lance Agent

THE ship from Carthagena carried Neuhoff to a France nearing the last throes of a vast speculative boom. John Law, son of an Edinburgh goldsmith, mathematical genius and, like Neuhoff, an adventurer in his way, had persuaded the Regent of the merits of his "System". Establishing, first, a bank with note-issuing powers, and next, the great chartered trading *Compagnie des Indes*, the enterprising and sanguine Law had created, by 1719, an orgy of speculation. The *actions* of the company (nominal value 500 *livres*) were bid up, in the stock-jobbing Rue Quincampoix, to the fantastic figure of 12,000 *livres*.

It was a situation highly congenial to Neuhoff, with his old debts to meet in Paris, little in his pockets but a handful of stolen jewels, and his youthful passion for high play still at work. It was not difficult to meet Law, *cet écossais célèbre*; and the famous "charm" did the rest. Theodore was "let in" to the boom; and in that crazy speculation he could not go wrong. Mr Tilson's *Letter from Paris* records that Law helped Neuhoff, on his return from Spain, to make "*une Fortune des plus Brillantes*": not merely did he pay off his creditors, he was "*Plutus en chair et en os*". Certainly he had regained his self-confidence. As if the little affair of the

32

Knights of Malta had never existed, he had the effrontery to write to "Madame", suggesting that, in his new-found prosperity, he should re-enter her household. He got no answer; "Liselotte" was unforgiving. His pockets full of Law's banknotes, Theodore brushed the rebuff aside. But unhappily the boom was nearing collapse. By April 1720 the stock of the *Compagnie des Indes* was crashing downwards in the Rue Quincampoix; by June the selling had turned into panic. Ruined and discredited, Law left France, for exile, in October. The late summer of 1720 found Neuhoff "caught out" in the slump, and once more in dire financial straits.

He naturally appealed to his sister, the Comtesse de Trévoux, for aid and shelter. This, according to the *Letter from Paris*, she furnished "to the best of her ability"; and, if we are to believe "Madame", was requited scurvily by her brother for her hospitality. ("He has stolen from his sister all she had—200,000 francs. . . . He has now disappeared and his sister is in despair". *Letter of October 20, 1720.*) "Liselotte's" account of this theft from Elizabeth, however, is probably ill-founded slander: the man was sometimes painted blacker than he was. The British agent who wrote to Mr Tilson would surely have repeated the story if it had had any substance or even wide currency; and it hardly squares with the return of Neuhoff to Paris and the Trévoux *hôtel* in 1727.

On the evidence of the agent, Neuhoff fled from Paris in 1720 simply to escape imprisonment for debt. His sister, he writes ("no more chaste than her brother"), had a lover, the Comte de la Marck. Jealous of the "affection" (the agent's implication is salaciously pejorative) bestowed by Elizabeth on her brother, the count suggested to Theodore's creditors that they should procure a "*lettre de cachet*"—a writ from which there was no appeal, no escape—against him.

This particular smear can be dismissed as Genoese calumny, invented years later. Battistella (*Il Re Teodoro*, 1890) observes that a senior officer of the Régiment de la Marck—brother-in-law of the Comtesse d'Apremont—was a frequent guest at the Trévoux table in 1720. He met there (in amity, it seems) the black sheep of the family, Baron Theodore. That Elizabeth had incestuous relations* with her brother, or that she had a lover, or knew anybody called "La Marck" is quite unproven.

The debt crisis of Theodore in the autumn of 1720, however, was all too serious. In the letter already quoted, "Madame" writes that she met Neuhoff in October, on her way to the Carmelite church. "Look," she said, "there's honest Neuhoff, come to pay his debts." He turned "white as a sheet". "Madame" may have exaggerated the basilisk power of her reproachful glance; but Theodore, after the collapse of the "Mississippi" boom, was understandably at his wits' end. However, his training under Görtz and Alberoni—with some useful commercial advice, the previous autumn, from Ripperdà—suggested a way out. If the Jacobite cause was dead—and so it must have seemed in 1720—he had knowledge to sell, knowledge, for instance, of many private and compromising letters exchanged between Alberoni and Victor Amadeus of Savoy, which the Emperor would like to read. Leaving Paris hurriedly for The Hague, he established himself there as a diplomatic "private eye", a free-lance entrepreneur of espionage.

According to the 1743 pamphlet, he had already learned during 1720 in Paris "how to give Ministers lights which

---

* On May 28, 1736, the *Daily Post* published prominently a letter from "one who knew Neuhoff abroad in 1719", defending the baron and his sister from "such calumnies". Was it not true, asked the writer, that "most princes had sallies in their youth"? But the baron had "fine accomplishments, embellished by an inexhaustible fund of good nature". The writer was a little indiscriminate in his defence of a rogue; but incest did not figure among Theodore's sins. The Genoese created a mythical "Comte de la Marck" from the name of a regiment!

they wanted, and drew thereby the necessary supplies for his wants"—no bad description of a spy who had kept copies of useful correspondence. Unfortunately, apart from nasty threats by his creditors, this business of "giving lights" had made Paris distinctly dangerous for the baron. The agents of Turin, for instance, had knives. Holland was safer—and a good place to borrow money in. At The Hague, his first step was to get into contact with the Emperor's Envoy to the States General. Through him, he forwarded to Zinzendorf, chancellor to Charles VI, a report on Spanish intentions and the approaches made by Philip V to Victor Amadeus (it is to be feared that, in this deal, Theodore was disloyal both to Alberoni and Ripperdà) whose value, in its recipient's eyes, seems to have been considerable. At any rate Zinzendorf forwarded 5,000 florins as payment for the information.

Alas, espionage and the sale of "lights", without a steady protective patron, is a precarious profession. The "free-enterprise" diplomatic business established at The Hague lacked steady, paying clients. Mr Tilson's Paris agent credits Neuhoff with having "made money" at that time from Portuguese Jews in Amsterdam; and later events suggest that he then established business contacts with these commercial circles. He certainly borrowed money from them. Nevertheless, hard times fell on Theodore in those years.

He had, however, a brash resiliency which makes him (you might say) of one kind with the Russian exiles, after the revolution of 1918, who drove taxis and ran night-clubs. For two years in The Hague he lived by his wits. He gave lessons in music; performed, as "virtuoso", at some concerts; posed as "chymist"—for what dubious purposes one can but guess; passed as an "expert" in art. (His fees were proportioned to clients' credulity, and he sold some very questionable Old Masters to the good citizens of Rotterdam and Amsterdam.) And then? A veil descends. In Zinzendorf's (probably irregular) pay, and as a fairly high-level travelling spy, he did "confidential jobs" from one end of the Continent to the other. He was always reticent about his doings in 1723-4, and the chronology of his movements is obscure; but, when no business fell his way, he would retire for a time to Cologne, where food and shelter were always available in the lodging of his cousin, Baron von Drost, now Grand Commander of the *Deutsche Ritter*.

Having thus "disappeared" for two years, Theodore next emerges in Rome. There, in 1725, masquerading under the title of Baron Stephan Romberg, he made the acquaintance of two charitable *religieuses*, sisters by the name of Fonseca, in the convent of Saints Dominique et Sixte. To them Neuhoff revealed his real name. They were kind to him— an odd attitude, come to think of it, on the part of two elderly nuns towards a shady young adventurer. (One must presume that the *"douceur"* of which Mr Tilson's agent wrote, was operative.) Theodore told the Fonsecas that the alias was necessary because he was in Rome "on business". In fact, the free-lance espionage industry had looked up. In 1724, Ripperdà, now Chief Minister at Madrid, had journeyed to Vienna in the hope of negotiating a Spanish-Austrian *entente* based on inter-family marriages and the promise of Spanish aid to the Empire against the Turks. The Infant Carlos was to marry the Archduchess Maria Theresa of Austria, and his younger brother, Philip, her sister. A pretty scheme, for which it was sought to secure the favour of the Pope, on the ground that one of the ultimate objectives of this new Catholic Bloc would be the restoration of the faith in England.

Sitting, hands in empty pockets, before the Grand

Commander's fire in Cologne, Theodore had got, just before Christmas 1724, an unexpected letter. It was from Zinzendorf, enclosing a banker's draft. Was Neuhoff free to execute a commission? If so, he was to go to the Holy See, and renew his acquaintance with "James III". He was to find out discreetly how James stood with the Pope, and what news from Scotland was reaching Rome. Was it true that the Disarming Act of 1716 had been largely ineffectual in the Highlands, and that the Lowlands were protesting riotously against the new malt duty imposed in 1724? Neuhoff must sift all the tidings from Edinburgh, and report. Alberoni, too, was now in the Holy City; and his advice regarding the Stuart cause should be sought.

Taking a gaily nonchalant leave of his cousin, Neuhoff was off to Rome without delay. There he busied himself conspiratorially in the entourage of James Edward, and could be seen hurrying importantly up the back stairs of the Vatican. He was thirty-one, a fine figure of a "gentleman adventurer" in his prime. His "progress reports" to Zinzendorf were enthusiastic: the Jacobites, he wrote, were spoiling for the fray, the Pope was sympathetic, Alberoni cautious but very friendly. None of this was well-founded "intelligence", but Theodore liked to please his clients. He sent his best respects to Ripperdà.

That genial, sanguine Dutchman, who was soon to overreach himself badly, had, in fact, forgiven Neuhoff for the little matter, in 1719, of the misappropriated "recruiting" funds. Theodore, he thought, could still be useful. That autumn he had not merely secured the Emperor as ally—getting a dukedom as his reward—but he had neatly exploited the Alliance of Hanover (September 3) in which England, France and Prussia engaged themselves to "maintain the Balance of Power". Making capital out of this challenge from the north, Ripperdà persuaded the Emperor to agree (with some reservations) to the proposed betrothals. Jubilant, he hurried back to Madrid.

Boasting, with no justification, that the Emperor was pining to hurl George I from his throne in London, Rip-perdà now began actively to revive Alberoni's schemes for another Stuart *coup* against England: troops were drilled, the northern Spanish ports put on a war footing. Ormond, old now and tired; the foppish Duke of Liria, Marshal Berwick's son; Wharton, with his pipe and his bottle—all these romantic and ineffectual figures sat plotting in Madrid during the winter of 1725–6,while English ships patrolled the Channel and blockaded the Spanish Indies. One of their company, back in Ripperdà's favour, Neuhoff—after the precarious years of free-lance espionage—enjoyed thoroughly the congenial job of acting as paid courier between Madrid and Rome. There were, even in those days, elastic expense accounts.

In Italy, he had time for interests outside professional "secret service" work. According to a French naval apothecary-doctor[14] who visited Corsican waters in 1738, Neuhoff made the acquaintance, during his visits to Rome in 1725–6, of a monk who dealt in magic and was hot on the search for the Philosopher's Stone. This was a ploy quite to the taste of the man who had made money in Holland by his talents in "chymistry". Magic, so he said to himself, might always come in useful. Meanwhile, there were the handy fees from Ripperdà and Zinzendorf.

Unhappily for Theodore, these were destined soon to end. Early in 1726, Marshal Konigsegg arrived in Madrid as the Emperor's Envoy, and lost little time in convincing Philip and Queen Elizabeth that Ripperdà had lied grossly in depicting Charles VI as being eager to fight the new Triple Alliance. Disgraced, and imprisoned for a time in Segovia, Ripperdà contrived his escape; and, in company

with a mistress, Doña Josepha Ramos, fled, *via* Portugal
and Ireland, to London. There, ingratiating himself with
the Government by his readiness to "spill the beans" about
secret clauses attached to the previous year's Treaty of
Vienna, he lived grandiosely for some years in Soho Square.
Later, after a brief stay in Holland, still rich and enjoying
life to the full, he went to Morocco, where we shall meet
him again in Neuhoff's story.

With his two good clients out of the picture, Neuhoff
hung about Rome for some months, borrowing from the
kind *religieuses*. At the end of 1726 he went back to Paris,
and became the guest once more of his sister. It was not an
agreeable visit. Trévoux was inclined now to look askance
at his dubious brother-in-law; and Paris was uncomfort-
ably full of unpaid and revengeful creditors. Theodore cut
his stay short, and went to London. A gift from his sister
enabled him, at first, to lodge in some style at the Ipswich
Arms in Cullum Street, not far from the Tower. After
that he economized, reluctantly, in a humble coffee-house
which let cheap rooms. (According to the *Daily Journal*, it
was "Brown's", in Spring Gardens.) Credit was hard to
obtain. Though he managed to obtain small loans from
trusting merchants in the City, an attempt to raise capital
for the development of the Philosopher's Stone failed. Funds
grew very low, though he did what he could with his gifts as
"virtuoso, chymist and art expert". But it was a grey time
for the extravagant *ci-devant* gilded page of "Liselotte".

Courcillon and most of the useful friends of his youth
were dead or estranged; and, with the Hanoverian dynasty
firmly on the English throne, he cursed the years spent, under
Görtz and Alberoni, plotting Stuart restoration. What had
he got out of it? Ripperdà's house in Soho Square was
good for a free meal, now and then; but that shrewd
Dutchman would not make himself *persona ingrata* with the

authorities by having too much to do with his ex-agent in the world of espionage. His occasional guineas kept the wolf from Theodore's door; but creditors became inconveniently pressing: London was no place for a penniless foreigner. But where to go?

Paris and The Hague both being territory forbidden by the menace of unpaid debts, Theodore decided that Italy—cheaper and more indulgent to transgressors—offered the best prospects. Thither, with modest funds "borrowed" from Ripperdà, he went in the autumn of 1728; and for four years he led a roving, clandestine existence. Always at his wits' end for ready cash, more and more the "confidence trick" play-actor "crook", trading on a good appearance and a noble name, he masqueraded in this city and that as Baron von Naxaar, Baron von Smihmer, Baron von Nissen and Baron von Smitberg. Bigou and other kindred cut-throats were his companions.

In 1730 he turned up again in Rome, sponging on the Fonsecas and pretending to be the accredited agent of Duke Francis of Lorraine. Next year, in Venice, he gave it out, for the benefit of his inn-keeper, that he had letters from "James III" to the Doges. Turin he did not venture to visit; the Savoyards had grudging memories of his services to Zinzendorf. But Naples saw him more than once; and in the spring of 1732 he was back in Rome. There[15] he borrowed 175 *livres* from a M Poilvache of Liége, on the strength of a bond guaranteed by Canon Lers of Essen, whom the baron had interested in the famous Philosopher's Stone. The lender was never repaid by Neuhoff. Much later, he got his money back by seizing the horses of the canon, who imprudently put up at the "Black Eagle" inn on a visit to Liége, the creditor's home town—a *dénouement* at which Theodore, when he heard of it, laughed heartily.

It was a disreputable Odyssey for a German nobleman who had been the confidential emissary of Görtz and Alberoni, and had been on speaking terms with a Stuart "king in exile". Cheating the credulous with tales of the Philosopher's Stone (magic *had* come in useful), borrowing from the trusting and sponging on the charitable, Baron von Neuhoff was near to becoming, in those years, a vulgar swindler. When money came his way, by hook or crook (and it was mostly by a *tour d'escroc*), he did himself well: at thirty-eight there were bags under those deceptively candid, wide-open eyes of his. But there were often mean, shabby days when a remittance from Baron von Drost in Cologne had to be begged humbly to save the desperate situation.

The patent of nobility, real or assumed, was now Theodore's sole (and dwindling) asset. It was in the guise of an English lord (the title is unhappily unrecorded) that he came from Rome to Genoa in the early summer of 1732. Strolling from his lodging through the lanes and porticos near the harbour (Theodore had now a catholic taste in cheap women) the "English lord", turning a corner, bumped into a Franciscan lay brother. There were apologies, an invitation from Theodore to share a flask of wine, for which he hoped the monk would pay. The Franciscan—his name[16] was Ruffino—came from Farmiole in Corsica. He had a long and stirring tale to tell of his compatriot's struggle against Genoese tyranny. Neuhoff pricked up his ears; listened intently. From that chance acquaintance much was to follow. On the sordid theme of eighteenth-century roguery, this adventurer from Westphalia was to embroider an astonishing, romantic variation.

CHAPTER FOUR

Genoa's Distressful Island

SINCE 1729, said Ruffino, Corsica had been in active revolt against Genoese occupation. From 1567, when the nationalist movement headed by Sampiero of Bastelica was broken and Sampiero assassinated, the Republic of Genoa had ruled the island as a convenient colony for greedy Governors and hungry officials. Suppressed and powerless, embittered and revengeful (*"il corso non perdona mai né vivo né morto"*), the Corsicans throughout the seventeenth century had nursed their grievances and sought distraction from national wrongs in family and clan vendettas. The Genoese found it convenient to raise revenue from freely offered gun-licences: between 1710 and 1728 there were nearly a thousand assassinations annually in the island. It was all (reflected Neuhoff) a little like the contemporary history of Scotland. Still, the wine in the *cantina* was not bad, and he had time on his hands. He was ready to listen.

The last straw, the lay brother went on, had come three years ago. The harvest, never abundant, had been particu-larly bad; and frayed tempers in the island had been exacerbated by the news of a brutal incident[17] at Finale, in Liguria. A Corsican soldier in Genoese service, under-going field punishment (he had been set humiliatingly on a wooden horse), was mocked by a crowd of Italian peasants. Angered, his comrades had fired on the crowd, with fatal results: after summary court martial, several were executed. On top of this news came a Genoese decision to discontinue the licensing of guns and to make good the loss of revenue by a hateful tax of 12 *scudi* (so-called *"due seini"*, two sixes) on every hearth. A new, harsh Genoese governor, Felice Pinelli, ruled at Bastia; he ordered the hearth tax to be collected with vigour.

The spark which fired revolt was touched off, on October 30, at the village of Bozio, near Corte. There, said Ruffino, an old peasant, by name Cardone, was injuriously used because his purse, emptied for the tax-collector, included a clipped gold piece—half a *soldo* short-weight—in its contents. Pinelli's tax-collector, refusing to accept the coin, threatened Cardone with distraint and eviction. Full of his wrongs, the old peasant gathered round him in the village of Bustanica an excited crowd who swore they would pay no more taxes to Genoa. Apprised of this disturbance, and the news that conch-horns were being blown in the hills to assemble malcontents, Pinelli sent out a detachment of 100 soldiers from Bastia. At Poggio di Tavagna the troops were surprised in their sleep, disarmed and sent back to their master. Led, at first, by one Pompiliano of Poggio, an armed insurrection had begun.

It went well for the insurgents. The command passed to Andrea Colonna Ceccaldi of Vescovato, and Luigi Giafferi of Talasani. The fort of Montserrato was captured, the town of Aleria stormed, Bastia blockaded, Calvi and Ajaccio invested. Pinelli was recalled, in disgrace, and his successor, Camillo Doria, instructed to treat with the rebels. But they were in defiant mood. Demanding the repeal of all taxes and two million *scudi* in "reparations", they insisted that Corsicans must garrison Ajaccio and

Bonifacio, and that the island's government must include an elected Assembly. Doria would not accept these terms. Giafferi went to Tuscany in quest of aid and munitions of war; and a shrewd priest, Canon Orticoni, was sent to Rome to negotiate for the Pope's support.

"The Pope?" Theodore raised his eyebrows. He had seen something of Benedict XIII's entourage in the days when Ripperdà was backing the Jacobite cause, and knew that his successor, Clement XII, had a still more cautious diplomatic cabinet. They would not readily risk burning their fingers in a Corsican rebellion against Genoa. "Had Orticoni got anything out of his mission?"

"Well," replied Ruffino, "at least a blessing; one might say 'moral' support, no more."

Neuhoff shrugged his shoulders. He had heard something of recent doings by the powers in connection with Corsica.

Alarmed by the spread of the revolt, Ruffino continued, the Genoese Republic had complained to the Emperor that Spain was succouring the rebels. Charles VI, appreciating that Corsica might be a base for hostile operations against Austria's possessions in Italy, agreed—to the displeasure of the suspicious French Government—to provide assistance against the insurrection. Not without payment: Genoa, he insisted, must foot the military bill—4 florins a month per man, *plus* 100 florins per man killed. So, after haggling, a bargain was struck. On August 10, 1731, an Austrian force, 4,000 strong, operating at Genoa's expense, under General Baron von Wachtendonck, landed near Bastia and raised the siege of the town. Striking west and south, the Austrians relieved Calvi and Ajaccio.

To raise a siege was one thing; to crush the rebellion quite another. The insurgents retreated into the inaccessible mountains, and sent forth appeals to emigré patriots to

return. According to Ruffino, they flocked back; and in
what spirit! "Name of God! Was there not the case of
Feliciano Leoni and his father?" Landing[18] near St Florent,
this young Corsican, who had been serving as a captain in
the army of Naples, met his old parent leading a party to
assault the Genoese tower at Nonza. "Go in my stead," said
the patriarch, to whom, some hours later, a sorrowing
messenger brought the news that, though the tower had
fallen, Feliciano was dead. "The tower captured? Huzzah!
Evviva Corsica!" Thus did the father greet good news.

When James Boswell visited Corsica, thirty years later,
and complained in his *Journal* of the perilous mountain
tracks over which his donkey carried him, by the slippery
edge of shadowed, precipitous gorges, he was told that the
women of Corte, under the Genoese domination, had
refused to marry lest they give birth to slaves. Such was the
temper of the Resistance. An earlier eighteenth-century
English pamphlet[19] described the Corsicans of Neuhoff's
day as a "brave . . . rough and stubborn" lot. Their
stubborn bravery was helped by geography. The central
chain of Corsican mountains runs up to 9,000 feet; its
lower slopes are a wilderness of cliffs and *maquis*—prickly
cystus, lentisk and arbutus. Even today an unwary walker
who leaves the known paths is entangled in impassable
rocks and giant heath, in which a hillside could hide a
regiment of soldiers.

Two centuries ago, as they strove to pacify the *maquis*,
Wachtendonck's pursuing columns suffered badly in
ambushes amid those rocks—notably near San Pellegrino
—and a force led by Doria was cut up at Calenzana, near
Calvi, by rebel bands who hurled beehives (full of furious
bees) at the enemy when powder ran out. Headquarters'
reports to Genoa and the Emperor were discouraging, and
the Republic—its mercantile senators groaning at the cost

of colonial wars—was compelled to put up more money for
more mercenary assistance. In April 1732 a further 6,000
men, commanded by Prince Ludwig von Württemberg,
reached the island and drove the rebels deep into the barren
mountains.

Prince Ludwig, anxious to be quit of a tiresome assign-
ment in a "barbarous" island far from Vienna, proposed an
amnesty. Parleys were held at Corte, between Doria, acting
on the Republic's behalf, and a delegation on the rebel
side consisting of Luigi Giafferi (he made a resounding
"nationalist" speech), Andrea Ceccaldi, Simon Raffaelli,
Charles Alessandrini and Evariste Piccioli. Terms were
agreed—a general amnesty; all tax-arrears to be remitted;
Corsicans to be eligible for all administrative offices; a
board to be established to take cognizance of offences by
public officials; an advisory council of twelve (Corsicans)
to sit with the governor.

On these terms, which they thought (erroneously) to be
guaranteed by the Empire, the insurgents laid down their
arms. Prince Ludwig, with most of the Austrian troops,
left for Genoa, where the Senate, grumbling that the
Emperor's aid had cost them 30 million *livres*, nevertheless
gave the victorious general a magnificent banquet. But
the Genoese, flushed with their bought victory, over-played
their hand. Suspecting that the insurgents had sympathizers
in Genoa—the rich Genoese banker, Lanfranchi, was
believed to be on the rebel side—they tried to arrest Simon
Raffaelli's brother, Marco Antonio, in whose possession
they believed they would find incriminating documents.
Marco Antonio fled to the mountains; and, in retaliation,
Genoese police arrested, as hostages, his brother Simon,
together with Giafferi, Ceccaldi and a priest, Simon
Aitelli. The prisoners were lodged in jail—first at Bastia,
then Savona, on the mainland.

All this, between glass and glass of wine, was related by Brother Ruffino to Neuhoff, that night in the grimy *cantina* near the harbour of Genoa. From time to time in the narra‑ tion, Theodore had edged his stool a little away: fleas could jump; and a lay brother's cassock was suspect. But Brother Ruffino had made a positive suggestion: could not Neuhoff contribute to the success of the insurrection? His reaction was what one might expect from an experienced diplo‑ matic agent. One does not, he said, "sing canticles in Babylon": the city of Genoa was not a healthy place for too much talk about Corsican rebels and their plans. However, Leghorn was neutral, even friendly towards the Corsicans; he (Neuhoff) was going there; and, if there were "interested parties" in Leghorn, well, "one would see. . . ."

At this stage, in the winter of 1732–3, Neuhoff's pre‑ liminary contacts at Leghorn with Canon Orticoni and the other Corsican representatives were cautiously explorative. Later, as we shall see, he claimed that he had long been "at great expense" in trying to help the Corsicans, but this was one of Theodore's calculated lies. His highly unreliable biographer, "Colonel Frederic", declares that, on hearing of the arrest of the four Corsican leaders, Neuhoff went magnanimously to Vienna and persuaded the Emperor to "make the Genoese feel the blackness of their crime". This action, says Frederic, convinced the Corsicans of "the greatness of his soul". A touching tribute from a man who pretended falsely to be Theodore's son; but the truth is that, in the winter of 1732, Neuhoff was much less altruistically engaged, though it is probable that he subsequently claimed credit, as Chevrier alleges, for the Emperor's intervention.

In fact, having gone to Leghorn, he got himself into a thoroughly bad scrape. Posing as the titled representative of Dutch business interests, he succeeded in ingratiating himself with a German banker, Franz Anton Jabach of

Cologne, who had a Livornese business. Jabach lent Neuhoff the considerable sum of "515 gold pieces", which was not repaid when the note-of-hand fell due. The banker prosecuted: Neuhoff was jailed; but—falling sick in prison —he was transferred to hospital and subsequently released. Jabach, who was leaving Leghorn for his home in Germany, relented and withdrew his charge of "false pretences". Not, one would say, an episode conducive to the credit of the future claimant to a crown. There is no reason, however, to credit Theodore, at this stage, with regal ambitions. He had indeed begun to wonder if money could not be made out of the island. He had learnt from Görtz that rebellions could be turned to profitable account. But before the idea of capitalizing monarchy was born in his fertile brain, much had happened in Corsica.

The plight of the imprisoned patriots had aroused sympathy abroad. In England, *Fog's Journal* had advertised their wrongs: "Every Friend of Liberty must wish the Corsicans to be established in the Natural Freedom of Mankind." Louis XV had interceded on their behalf with Doria, the Genoese Envoy in Paris; and Prince Eugène of Savoy had made representations to the Genoese Senate. At length, on April 22, 1733, the four were released, and on May 8 they formally made submission to the Senate and received their pardon. Simon Raffaelli went to Rome, where he employed himself in the service of the Vatican. His brother, Marco Antonio, secured a post in the secretariat of the Grand Duke of Tuscany. Giafferi—as compensation presumably for injustice—was appointed, at a handsome salary, as Vice-Commandant of Savona. Ceccaldi went to Spain, and Aitelli to Leghorn. The Emperor ordered the recall of Wachtendonck and the remaining mercenaries.

In Corsica, however, a fresh storm was soon to gather. A new governor, Paolo Pallavicino, described by a contemporary Corsican historian[20] as "a scourge of men", ruled in Camillo Doria's stead; and his régime was based on wholesale preventive jailing of "suspects". Following the arrest of several members of the Ciavaldini family, the early months of 1734 saw a new insurrection which began at Rostino and was led by Giacinto Paoli (father of Pasquale Paoli, famous a generation later) with Giacomo Castagnetta as his chief lieutenant. Other chiefs in the rising were Ginastro, Gentili, Luc Ornano and Maldini. Giafferi, abandoning his salary at Savona, hurried back to the island in the company of Sebastiano Costa, a clever Corsican who had been a lawyer in Genoa and of whose constitution-drafting we shall later hear much. Andrea Ceccaldi returned from Spain and Aitelli from Leghorn, to join the rebel leadership. Corte was taken by assault; and Canon Orticoni was sent off on a new diplomatic mission—not to the Pope this time, but (with more material ends in view) to Philip V in Madrid. Genoa sent two commissioners, Fiesco and Giustianini, to try to negotiate a truce; but the rebels' temper was such that they hanged one Corsican found to be "in correspondence" with the commissioners, who returned to Genoa, their mission unaccomplished.

It was the news (which he got from a later meeting in Leghorn with Brother Ruffino) that Spain was being urged to take a hand in Corsican politics, which finally aroused Neuhoff's interest in the island. Orticoni failed to get any assurances of help from Madrid, and returned to Leghorn. This port—readily accessible by small boats from the island—became the mainland headquarters of the rebel leadership, and Neuhoff, released from jail *via* hospital, had long, conspiratorial discussions with Giafferi and Aitelli when they came to Leghorn to confer with Orticoni. The talks were joined, at that time, by Domenico Rivarola, who had formerly been Spanish consul at Leghorn, and was now acting, like Orticoni, as agent for the revolutionaries.

In these discussions Neuhoff had to play a difficult role. Since the Corsicans knew all about the regrettable Jabach business, he could not pose as a man of great personal possessions. What he could do was to make much of his "connections"—with Madrid and Vienna, with Alberoni, with Ripperdà and Duke Francis of Lorraine, with wealthy bankers in London and Amsterdam. The Corsicans were in urgent need of arms. "Who better placed than I", said Neuhoff, "to organize supplies from friendly quarters abroad?" In short, it was as a gun-runner that Neuhoff then persuaded the Corsicans to accept him as an associate. His services, at first, were useful, rather than glorious; he became a sort of commercial agent for the Resistance. The 1743 pamphlet records that "all this time [1734-5] he was in Portugal, Sicily or the Tuscan coasts, executing commissions and marketing, better than ever before, the commodities of Corsica". Why not? Acting as *commis voyageur* for a peasant rebellion may have been an odd job for a German baron; but had not Ripperdà himself done well politically out of skilful management of a factory?

Theodore's activities in those years were afterwards described dramatically, but with no truth or plausibility, by "Colonel Frederic". According to his account, having nobly espoused the insurgents' cause, Theodore went to Rodosto, to consult with "his friend", Rakoczy, the ex-Prince of Transylvania. There, we are asked to believe, Neuhoff unfolded an ambitious plan for a Moslem conquest of Italy—with a Turkish sea-borne invasion from the east supported by the North African Moors, who would seize Corsica as a base. Delighted with this brilliant scheme, Rakoczy is supposed to have sent Neuhoff to Constantinople with a warm letter of recommendation to Osman

Pasha, Comte de Bonneval, who "approved" and wafted the baron on to Tunis with "large sums" of money from the Port's exchequer and an official letter of introduction to the Bey.

Alas! This colourful Odyssey was an invention of Theodore's or the child of "Colonel Frederic's" imagination. Rakoczy (even supposing that Neuhoff had ever met him) was then an old, dying man, and Bonneval was no fool: he would have had nothing to do with such a crack-brained scheme presented by a penniless Westphalian adventurer. Neuhoff's activities were much less glamorous. His new clients in the Corsican Resistance had few enough commodities whose export called for their magnificent agent's marketing skill. But some cargoes they contrived; some money, for the purchase of arms, they managed to raise; and Theodore journeyed, more than once, to the Levant, bartering olive oil and wine for guns. His heart was never wholly in this humdrum job of bargaining for arms; but beggars, even with a patent of nobility, cannot be choosers; and when he needed an excuse for slow execution of a commission, he pleaded that he had had "good hopes" of raising funds, or obtaining muskets on credit, from Smyrna.

After one such voyage to the Levant, in the autumn of 1734, the delay in his return was due to the compelling attractions of a *comprador's* young daughter in Palermo. Had it not been amusing to borrow from her uncle the price of that diamond brooch which demolished, like Jericho's trump, the walls of virtue? Neuhoff returned to Leghorn in happy mood. He had sold his cargo to Sicilian Jews, and had cash—less, of course, his personal "rake-off"—for the Corsican rebels in his pocket: a Florentine, whom he had recruited for the business, could turn the money into ammunition. Seeking Orticoni, he found him in glum

conclave with Giafferi and Rivarola. Brother Ruffino had
gone to Genoa—a rash journey—and had been arrested by
the *sbirri* of the Republic.

"A misfortune," said Neuhoff, shrugging his shoulders.

But that was not the sum of the insurgent leaders' worries.
Paoli was insanely brave, but reckless; Gentili and Luc
Ornano blew hot and cold. Aitelli and Castagnetta were
at daggers drawn. The whole integrity of the rebellion was
in danger of petering out in feuds. Nothing could save the
situation, said Giafferi, but a powerful reinforcement of
supplies—above all, some cannon—and a leadership which
the warring chiefs would accept. Rivarola nodded his head.

Was that meant, at this date, in the autumn of 1734, as
an invitation to Theodore? Unlikely. The Corsicans' idea
then was that Don Carlos of Naples might accept the
"protectorate" of Corsica. But they certainly hoped that
Theodore might some day succeed—had he not boasted of
his powerful connections?—in securing, on credit, a really
worthwhile cargo of munitions of war.

The wine of Leghorn was potent; and Neuhoff was
never slow to make promises. "Tomorrow," he said, "I'll
take ship for Tunis: the Bey is my good friend, and I have
letters to him from Gian Gastone de' Medicis,[21] Grand
Duke of Tuscany. Give you good night, gentlemen." With
a slight, but not unbecoming lurch in his gait, Neuhoff
took himself to his lodging and (on this occasion) celibate
bed.

There were delays before the glowing promise that aid
would be sought from the Bey was fulfilled. Theodore did
not propose to arrive in Tunis empty handed: he must have
funds to establish his standing there. Raising the money
took time: Giafferi and Orticoni could do little to help.
Eventually, on the pretext that Livornese slaves would be
purchased in Tunis, the Leghorn Jews[22] were induced to

lend the Corsicans' emissary 4,000 *livres*. But some intro⁄
ductions to a strange city would also be useful. The Jews
obliged, and so, after a little persuasion, did H.M. Consul
in Leghorn. Partly because, like many Englishmen of the
day, he sympathized with the Corsican rising, partly
because he found Neuhoff an amusing rogue over a glass of
wine, he wrote a "commendatory letter" to his opposite
number, the British Consul in the Bey's city.

There Theodore arrived by ship, in March 1735. His
arrival was inconspicuous, but was noted by two Corsicans
from Bonifacio, by name Varalzi and Varsi. Slaves in
Barbary at the time, and employed in the habour of Tunis,
they were liberated a year later—no thanks to Theodore!
—and told their story to the authorities in Genoa. (Their
depositions survive in the State Archives.) They related
that Neuhoff disembarked and went to the house of one Dr
Leonardo Buongiorno. He, as we shall see, was an appro⁄
priate host for his adventurer⁄guest.

CHAPTER FIVE

The Arrival of the Liberator

IN Corsica, meanwhile, there had been stirring developments. By the end of 1734 most of the interior of the island
was in rebel hands: the Genoese forces were bottled up in
the garrison towns and a few isolated towers. The insurgents'
leaders—one detects the inspiration of the busy lawyer,
Sebastiano Costa—decided that it was time to give the
Nationalist Movement a constitutional form. At the beginning of 1735, Giafferi, Ceccaldi and Paoli (who, it will be
recalled, had started the revolt at Rostino) convened a
General Assembly of the patriots at Corte. This gathering,
on January 30, formally proclaimed "New Laws for the
Kingdom and Republic of Corsica"—an enactment which
combined a singular blend[23] of democracy and clannish
feudalism. The chief provisions of the Assembly's resolu-
tions were:

(1) That all the laws and statutes of Genoa be abrogated
and publicly burned.

(2) That all legislative power be derived henceforth
from an elected Assembly.

(3) That the supreme executive authority be a Council
of Twelve.

(4) That Andrea Ceccaldi, Luigi Giafferi and Giacinto
     Paoli be designated "*Primati*", with the title of
     "Highness". (Death was exacted as a penalty for
     "disrespect" to these personages!)

(5) That parliamentary control of the military leaders
     be exercised by a Committee of Six, nominated by
     the Assembly.

(6) That the Assembly appoint a Council of Four to
     supervise finance and justice.

(7) That, in default of succour from Spain, Corsica be
     placed under the protection of the Blessed Virgin
     Mary, whose effigy should be borne on the national
     arms and flag.

A nineteenth-century German traveller[24] records that
during his visit to Bastia in 1852 he was allowed to read
(but not to copy) the MS of *Memorials of Corsica* written by
one Accinelli in 1736-7. Accinelli, who was evidently a
propagandist for Genoa, described the Corsicans of the day
as a "*generatio prava et exorbitans*—pigs and beasts, one and
all". Such a description was scarcely merited by a people
who may have been largely unlettered, but yet voted a
constitution which, for the times, was not illiberal. The
trouble was that, as in contemporary Scotland, family feuds
were rife in the insurgents' ranks; and even in the leadership
there were jealousies—destined later to play a significant
part in Neuhoff's fortunes. Paoli resented the fact that
Giafferi had returned from the mainland to share in the
leadership of the revolt which he, Paoli, had started; and he
was jealous, too, of Ceccaldi.[25] The priest, Aitelli, also
disliked the better-educated Costa; and there were continual
quarrels between local chiefs in the *maquis*.

As the year 1735 wore on, the position of the insurgents
grew difficult. They had insufficient armaments to storm

the strong towns of Bastia, Calvi and Ajaccio, and the sea-
blockade of the island by Genoese warships was beginning
to result in a grave shortage of food supplies. In the summer
the Republic of Genoa dispatched the (now pardoned)
former governor, Pinelli, to Corsica with reinforcements of
troops and orders to suppress the rising at all costs. He
nearly succeeded in capturing Costa at Giafferi's house
near San Pellegrino; but his troops made little headway in
the mountains. As General Wachtendonck had found, a
hillside of almost impenetrable thorny scrub could hide
500 men, and ambushes were deadly. Nevertheless, the
rebels were becoming desperate for lack of bread and
powder.

It seems likely that the rebellion might have collapsed
that autumn but for the unexpected arrival near Ile Rousse
of two small ships which brought supplies from "English
sympathizers". (No more is known of this odd incident,
save that the ships' masters would accept nothing but a
glass of wine each.) Thus reprieved from the immediate
threat of starvation, the rebels renewed their activity: they
invested Calvi and Bonifacio more closely; captured the
town and port of Aleria; and succeeded in burning the
Bishop's Palace at Ajaccio.

Counsels, however, remained divided; there was an
extreme "nationalist" group, led by Astaldi, who disapproved of Orticoni's appeals for foreign aid, and many of
the rebel chiefs favoured an endeavour to come to terms with
Pinelli. Indeed, in February 1736 they offered a truce if
Genoa would renounce her "prerogatives" in Corsica, and
reduce her garrison to an agreed level. The Republic
declined; and a "strong" governor, Paolo-Battista Rivarola,
was sent to rule at Bastia.

So much for the course of events in the island. Established
in March 1735, at Tunis, Neuhoff lost no time in presenting

his introduction to Mr Lawrence, the British consul, and in interesting his host, Leonardo Buongiorno, in his plans. These he disclosed gradually, with circumspection. Ostensibly, as we have seen, he had come to Tunis in order to negotiate the ransoming (*rachat*) of Livornese captured at sea and enslaved by the Bey; and for this pur-pose he professed to have large credits available in Leghorn. Buongiorno smiled politely—with a doubt in his mind. The repurchase of slaves was nominally his own concern, too, in Tunis; but, according to the Varalzi–Varsi depositions already quoted, this none too scrupulous Sicilian had embezzled the funds given him for the purpose by the Sicilian Government, and had set himself up in Tunis as a doctor. With the practice of medicine he combined other interests, including the collection of all "intelligence" likely to be useful to Don Carlos of Naples; and he had already heard tales of Theodore's "commercial" activities on behalf of the Corsican rebels. "Was his quest concerned solely with slaves?" The question was accompanied by a wink.

Shedding his pose of haughty altruism—he sensed that in Buongiorno he had met a bird of his own feather—Neuhoff revealed the real nature of his mission. Could the Bey be persuaded to back the Corsicans with a substantial reinforcement of arms—not forgetting the precious cannon those fire-eaters wanted for the bombardment of the Genoese towers? Buongiorno was sceptical: what could the Bey expect to get out of it? But help might perhaps be procured on a lower level. He would invite two friends to his house that evening.

The doctor's invited guests proved to be the Bey's treasurer and, surprisingly, the director of the Spanish hospital in Tunis—another *medico* with subterranean political interests. Under a tree in Buongiorno's shady garden this oddly assorted quartet sipped mint-tea and discussed ways and means. The Spaniard undertook, not very hopefully, to write to Madrid. More constructively, the treasurer thought he saw his way to a fair supply of arms—including those cannon!—if there were money to pay for them. That was the difficulty. More long talks followed, next day and later. Mr Consul Lawrence was invited to take tea (Neu‑ hoff had brought with him a generous consignment of Rhine wine, but the treasurer had strict religious views) and lent his counsel. But he had no funds. "What about the Greek and Jewish traders in Tunis?" The suggestion was Neuhoff's; but the others agreed that there might be some‑ thing in it.

Theodore had his letters from the Jews in Leghorn. Accompanied by Buongiorno he went the rounds of the *souk*—a remarkable figure in the traders' unostentatious places of business. They quickly made it evident that they would be prepared to help finance a venture to Corsica— but on two conditions. Neuhoff must be in a position to guarantee them trading concessions in the island, and the whole scheme must be "underwritten" by a powerful backer. This, for Theodore, presented a problem: he had no status in the government of "free" Corsica, and he had little hope of getting any official backing either from Madrid or Don Carlos. More conclaves followed in Buongiorno's garden, more mint‑tea was sipped—until Neuhoff had an idea: he remembered Ripperdà.

Having tired of London and, still more, of his native Holland, Baron Ripperdà had gone, in 1732, to Morocco. He was not the only European immigrant to find favour with Sultan Muley Abdulla. Among the "renegades", as they were then called, an Irish adventurer by the name of Carr was at that time the superintendent of the cannon factory at Mekèns, where Ripperdà at first went. Converted—at least officially—to Islam, the baron had commanded the sultan's troops in operations against the Spaniards at Ceuta, was given the title of Effendi, and later settled down in rich and honourable retirement at Tetuan.

Thither, with a safe conduct provided by the Bey's treasurer, Theodore proceeded; and, to his relief, was hospitably received. His old ex-employer listened sympathetically to the tale of Corsican wrongs and Genoese oppression, though he shook his head when asked to "underwrite" the venture. According to the *Memoirs*[26] of Ripperdà, the Dutchman "felt great zeal" to aid his one-time agent. The "great zeal" may be doubted: but that rich and cynical old statesman, in his leisurely retirement, derived amusement from backing Neuhoff with some money and advice in an enterprise calculated to set all the powers at loggerheads. Indeed it was in Tetuan that the idea was born of doing more than merely run guns for the Corsican rebels. It was there that the plan was hatched that Theodore should make a bid for the crown of Corsica, and so put himself in a position to guarantee the Tunisian merchants a return for money invested. The notion would have appealed to Ripperdà's sense of humour.

During his stay in North Africa, negotiating for arms and money, Neuhoff was constantly in touch with Giafferi and Orticoni. In the summer and autumn of 1735 he had learned of the inter-clan quarrels and divided counsels in the island. They served him as text for a plausibly argued letter which he dispatched from Tetuan. If the Genoese could be defeated by an ample reinforcement of munitions and gold, would it not be sensible to avoid the dissipation of victory in internecine disputes? Why not choose a well-born, well-connected and meritorious non-Corsican associate as ruler? Such was the line of reasoning put by Neuhoff to Giafferi; and its receipt led to much Corsican head-scratching.

It will always remain a mystery how Theodore succeeded in "putting himself over" to the Corsicans—if indeed they ever took quite seriously the idea that a notorious adventurer should found a dynasty in their island. If we are to believe an almost contemporary account,[27] the more intelligent of the insurgents' leaders accepted Theodore only as a figure-head. They needed *"quelque chose qui fit du bruit"*, a "sensation" to spur laggards from defeatism, and to demonstrate to the whole world that Corsica would accept aid even from the Moors or the devil rather than submit to Genoa. All the same, I think it is clear that Theodore succeeded in estab-lishing, up to a point, some personal ascendancy over the partisans from the *maquis*; he had, as a French historian[28] has observed, *"assez la parole à la main"*, and the prestige of being Ripperdà's "friend" and guest—with access to the Dutchman's famous wealth—naturally helped. The Corsi-cans, moreover, were so desperate that they were ready to clutch at straws. As Filippini observed in his *Istoria di Corsica* (Pisa, 1827), *"Quando gli animi sono sollevati, è pronta la credenza ad ogni cosa"*. The helping hand is the hand of God.

With a purse of gold from Ripperdà in his bag, and an encouraging reply in his pocket from Giafferi to the sug-gestion of "election to the crown", Neuhoff returned to Tunis. There—partly on the strength of a guarantee from Buongiorno, but mainly on the false pretence that Ripperdà and the sultan himself were "committed" to the Corsican venture—he proceeded to borrow money on a substantial scale from Mordecai Senage and other wealthy Tunisian Jews. He was as good as crowned, he said: the trade of Corsica should be a Tunisian monopoly. Then came a stroke of luck. An English ship, whose master, by name Dick,[29] was the illegitimate son of Mr Consul Lawrence, turned up in the harbour, in January 1736.

Captain Dick was persuaded to convey Neuhoff to Corsica. The arms and stores procured through the Bey's treasurer with the borrowed money were loaded; an appropriate retinue was recruited; Oriental finery for the king was purchased; and on a fine March evening the ship sailed with Theodore—accompanied by Leonardo Buongiorno's brother, Christoforo—saluting from the poop in farewell, the British flag fluttering over his head.

The ship was barely out of the harbour when Leonardo Buongiorno put it about that the expedition was sponsored by Don Carlos of Naples. This "helpful" rumour, coupled with the news of the landing at Aleria, fluttered the chancelleries of Europe considerably. M de Campredon, the distinguished French Envoy in Genoa (where he had come from St Petersburg in 1727), was told by his government to secure full reports on developments in Corsica—a task which he passed on to the French vice-consul at Bastia, Signor d'Angelo; and Count Rivera, the Sardinian Envoy, was enjoined to use equal urgency in collecting news— which he did through his friendly relations with M de Campredon. Was England, or Spain, seeking to dominate the Mediterranean trade routes from a base in Corsica? Or was the sponsor of the enterprise Don Carlos, King of the Two Sicilies?

English embassies abroad were equally concerned to learn the truth—not least the envoy to the Emperor. Mr Robinson, at the Embassy in Vienna, received a confidential report[30] from Leghorn, dated April 4, which informed him of the landing in Corsica of an unknown person . . . "who stiles himself Viceroy of Corsica, Grandee of Spain, Prince of the Empire, English lord, Knight of the Golden Fleece, and Duke and Peer of France". We may suppose that Mr Robinson said "tut, tut", and waited for more reliable, more exact news. Gradually it came. By the end of

April the Amsterdam and London journals, after sensa-
tional rumours that the "stranger" was "a Swede", a
"Spaniard who never goes to Mass but without guards, nor
is served but in plate", were able to give their readers substantially the truth, though credence was still given to the
rumour that Neuhoff had landed with the backing of
"certain Powers". Here the Press, like the suspicious M
Campredon, erred. As we have seen, Theodore's backers
were at this stage a clique of speculative Greek and Arab
Jews in Tunis, whose itch for "value for money" he now
had to satisfy.

When the brigantine anchored off Aleria on March 12,
and was boarded by a party of patriots from the town, the
discussions which took place on board were protracted.
Disembarkation was postponed until a reply came to a
letter[31] which Theodore had drafted on the voyage and
now sent to Giafferi. It ran thus:

Most Illustrious Signor Giafferi,
At last I have reached the shores of Corsica, summoned
hither by your prayers and oft-repeated letters. The steadfast
love and fidelity shown by you and the Corsicans for over
two years has urged me to overcome my dislike of the sea and
my dread of the storms which are wont to rage at this time of
the year; but Heaven has hitherto blessed me and rendered
prosperous my voyages. I am here to give all succour in my
power to your oppressed kingdom and to liberate her, if God
so will, from the scourge of Genoa; and fear not that I shall
neglect in any way my duty to you who are faithful to me. If
you choose me as your king, I ask only the power to alter
one law—namely to grant liberty of conscience to men of
other nationalities and creeds who may come here to assist
our endeavours. Come, one and all of you to Aleria without
delay—Signori Costa, Paoli and others—that we may consult together to form our basis for action.
                                    Your devoted Theodore.

"Liberty of conscience"! A noble phrase, more noble than the truth, which was that Theodore had pledged to his Tunisian backers a monopoly of trading rights* in Corsica without fear of penalties for "infidels".

At this point a first-hand account of events becomes available from the pen of Sebastiano Costa, quondam practitioner in the law courts of Genoa. His account is partial, in the sense that he was, from first to last, Neuhoff's enthusiastic and devoted adherent; but there is no evidence to suggest that he was untruthful, and his *Diary*[32] constitutes the testimony of the man on the spot.

According to Costa, Giafferi's reaction to Theodore's letter was to bid Paoli, Giappiconi (another chieftain) and Costa meet him at Xaviero's house at Matra, in the foothills, about twelve miles from Aleria. Thither they all hurried—to find that the messenger who brought the letters had also brought some bottles of "real Rhine wine"—to aid, one imagines, the digestion of its contents—together with a present of "dates, *boutargues* [dried, smoked fish] and tongues" for Xaviero di Matra's wife.

Paoli, a rigid son of the Faith, had scruples, made difficulties about the "liberty of conscience" demand. It so happened, however, that an erudite churchman, Canon Albertini, happened to be staying at Matra. His advice was sought—and given in Theodore's favour. Did not the Holy Father permit Jews to trade and exercise their religion in Rome? Corsica was in dire straits; and the "stranger's" arrival, coinciding so nearly with the festival of the Assumption of the Blessed Virgin, had a flavour of Divine Providence in it: such a "miracle" had better be accepted on the

---

* On May 15, 1736, the London *Daily Journal* wrote: "We have it from good hands that the Viceroy of Corsica . . . has a project to make that Island the market-place of the Mediterranean . . . and to make all the Sea Ports free. . . . He is assisted by the Jews of Barbary with Money." The Press learned more than Theodore disclosed to the Corsicans.

terms offered. "In short," said the astute canon, "I believe this man to be a second Moses." So Paoli was over-ruled and sulkily accepted the majority decision—a new rift in the already uneasy relations between the leaders. Next morning, however, Paoli seems to have recovered his temper; for Costa records that, as the little band of patriots strode down the rough tracks towards Aleria, they sang—Paoli taking the lead with his prowess in improvising *ballades*.

At Aleria they had a friendly, courteous and impressive reception from Theodore, who now landed in their company and was lodged in a house in the town. An atmosphere of elegance was rapidly stage-managed. On tables covered with "snowy damask" a fine supper, with more Rhine wine and "exquisite dates", was served (Costa seems to have been by nature a *bon viveur*), and during the meal Theodore charmed the company with tales of his adventures. After supper, the baron made an appearance on a little balcony giving on the street; around him stood the Corsican chiefs, and on each side a Moorish slave held a blazing torch, while the crowd, gathered below, cheered lustily. Then more wine, more tales by Neuhoff.

> Wherein I spake of most disastrous chances,
> Of moving incidents by flood and field,
> Of hair-breadth scapes i' the imminent deadly breach,
> Of being taken by the insolent foe
> And sold to slavery, of my redemption thence
> And portance in my travels' history. . . .

We may be sure that Desdemona's father heard no more enthralling a history—interlarded, no doubt, with gossip of courts and royal favours. Costa, at any rate, was captivated; and the party went on till the sky over Italy was grey.

Next morning, Theodore kept to his bed until a late hour, and held a levée in his chamber, while "quaffing chocolate flavoured with rose-oil". What should be the next step? Some voices were raised in favour of the immediate election of the baron as King; but Theodore, says Costa, was "more prudent". His view was that there should be no precipitate action. He had written to other rebel leaders—Arrighi of Corte, and Fabiani of the Balagne, a fertile district round Ile Rousse. Their arrival should be awaited. Then "if they are of your opinion, let us continue this talk of matters of State". Meanwhile, Theodore suggested, a two-days' rest, while the ship discharged her cargo, would be no bad thing in view of the "heavy tasks ahead"; and he would like to take some walks in the country.

Presently he got up; and within half an hour had rejoined the patriots below—"right nobly attired, a perruque of the whitest hair, a vest of purple hue, a sword at his side, a cane in his hand and six attendants behind him, a knight of the chamber and three slaves". Addressing the chiefs with "the slightly distant graciousness that marks the manners of princes", he repeated firmly that he intended to explore, for a day or two, the sea-coast plain round Aleria. And this he did—shrewdly calculating that claimants to a crown, with so little title as he had to its possession, do well not to seem over-eager.

The tactic worked; the cargo came ashore. One contemporary report[33] relates that the ship proceeded to land "10 cannon, above 7,000 muskets, 2,000 pairs of shoes and 7,000 sacks of grain", together with bullion in the form of "Barbary gold and Tunisian *zecchini*"—to a total value of "2 million pieces of eight" (about £400,000). A later, less excited, chronicle[34] in 1770 scales down this list in some particulars: the "10 cannon" are accepted, but there were only 4,000 muskets and 700 sacks of grain; and, including the bullion, the total value of the store was "one million *scudi*". Even that figure (equivalent to £200,000) is in all

probability a wild exaggeration; the small ship could hardly
have held all that stuff. But no matter: the cargo was clearly
a valuable reinforcement for the rebels; indeed, the *London
Daily Post* later carried a dispatch from Marseilles that the
value of the "venture" was £100,000.

There was enough, at any rate, to excite the insurgents.
The crowd on shore grew enthusiastic as case after case
reached the harbour. There was a general distribution of
zecchini and Moorish shoes, which the poor Corsicans
thought "very fine"; and the people of Aleria, their numbers
swelled from neighbouring villages, began to shout "*Viva il
nostro Re!*" as Neuhoff passed by. Buongiorno discreetly
acted as cheer-leader.

CHAPTER SIX

The King is Crowned

By March 16 there was still no sign of Arrighi or Fabiani; and though the Genoese garrison of San Pellegrino had made no move, the fort was too near for Theodore's comfort in a town so open as Aleria: quarters nearer the sheltering *maquis* of the hills seemed prudent. So it was decided to move to the little hill-town of Cervione, some hours' march to the north. Mules had to be collected, with some difficulty, for Neuhoff's baggage and cases of wine; and the day began badly with a violent quarrel between Paoli's and Giafferi's followers over precedence in the line of march. Blows were struck, shots fired. Brandishing his cane, Neuhoff strode into the angry mob of partisans. "What means this folly? If I am to be your leader, it is I who shall settle questions of precedence, and distribute honours according to merit." Unless the aggressors in this faction-fight made amends by their immediate submission, the precious cargo would be re-embarked and the ship, with all his company, would sail from the island.

On this occasion the display of authority (however theatrical one may regard it) achieved results. Order was restored, and the cortège set out. But the departure had been so delayed by the fracas—an evil omen for days ahead—

that it was soon realized that Cervione could not be reached before nightfall. This did not suit Theodore's plans for a dramatic entry; and it was decided to bivouac for the night, half-way to Cervione, by a small river, the Bravone. The baron occupied a shepherd's hut; the rest slept under the stars, Costa comforted by "the plentitude of camp-fires" against the terrors of lonely night.

Next day, towards noon, Cervione was reached. One fancies that, by design, a messenger must have ridden ahead; for there were cheering crowds and a *feu de joie* so loud that the Genoese commandant at San Pellegrino, over six miles away, heard it with alarm and dispatched a *felucca* by sea to Bastia to report to the Governor that "something was afoot". Lodgings for the party had been prepared in the former Palace of the Bishop of Aleria, Monseigneur Mari. This comfortable Genoese prelate had left for the mainland two years ago, misliking the Corsican climate; and the Palace was empty and storm-blackened. Still, it served; and Theodore promptly sent forty men, with mules, to bring up four small cannon from Aleria. These he placed in front of the Palace, each with a sentinel—a pleasant, regal touch. (It took the whole population of Cervione, with mules and ropes, to haul the bigger guns up the hill next day.)

Meanwhile monks from several nearby monasteries arrived to welcome the "Liberator". The friendly Franciscans brought presents of oranges, lemons and wine which, Costa adds appreciatively, was "from the vintage of 1733". Only one thing marred the harmony of the arrival—a quarrel between the chiefs over the honour of occupying the room next to the baron's chamber. In this dispute, with or without Neuhoff's support, Paoli seems to have won.

It was not only the chiefs who quarrelled. Next day,

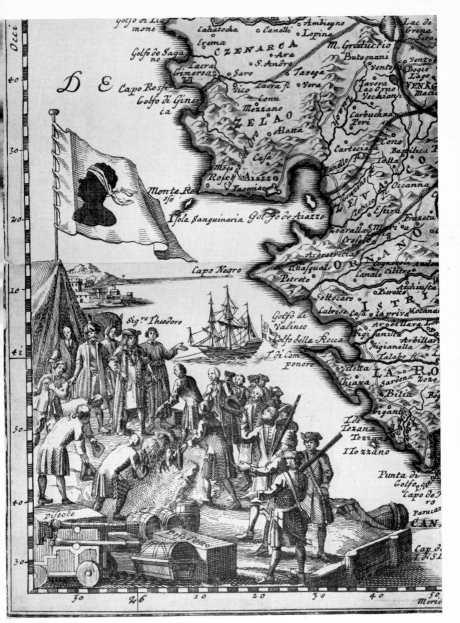

THE LANDING

Portion of map in *Das Alte und Neue Corsica*, Nuremburg, 1736

THEODORVS
L. B. de Neuhof.

THEODOR
Freyherr von Neuhof.

King Theodore in Glory
From an Engraving in the Bibliothèque Nationale, Paris

looking out from his window, Theodore witnessed a brawl between one of his Moors and a Corsican, who knocked the Moor out for the count. "*Was ist los?*" The indignant baron lapsed into German: he had the disorderly Corsican clapped in the cellars behind bars. An angry crowd of partisans gathered and demanded their comrade's release. So menacing grew the throng that the baron lighted a torch and, jumping on a powder-barrel, declared that he would blow the whole Palace to hell if discipline were not observed. Luckily his bluff was not called: some of the chiefs arrived and quenched the insubordination.

The incident, however, gave Theodore pause. He was a gambler; and though an eighteenth-century historian[35] describes him as "impetuous, quick in his designs but unable to carry them to a conclusion", he was not the man to abandon lightly a magisterial confidence trick which promised so much. But did he, even at this stage, begin to wonder if he could "pull it off" with the human material at his disposal? It seems likely. At all events he did a curious thing. Giving Paoli a present of 200 *zecchini* and appointing him Treasurer in Chief of the Army, with funds to give a small advance of pay to each new recruit, Theodore informed his "Court" that, since no serious operations against the Genoese could be begun until Captain Dick (whom he had sent to Leghorn) got back with more munitions, he proposed to spend a few "days of repose" at Matra in the company of Giafferi and Giappiconi.

Was this a device to separate quarrelling dogs? Did he think Paoli could get on with his job only if Giafferi were out of the way and could not interfere? It is possible. All the same, it struck even Costa as strange that Theodore should leave his headquarters at this early stage, before his position had been established, before any firm decision to crown him as king had been taken. He was indeed in an awkward situation: though the rebel chiefs had accepted his conditions about "liberty" for non-Catholic foreign mer-chants, a few days in Corsica had sufficed to disillusion him about the island's "export potential"; his backers in Tunis, he saw, had "backed a loser". That consideration alone would not have worried Neuhoff—he had cheated plenty of lenders before now—but if the warring clan-chiefs wrecked, between them, the whole plan of campaign— and the baron knew enough of soldiering to have little con-fidence in the few cannon he had brought from Tunis— was there not an unpleasant likelihood that the insurgents' "king" might end his days at the wrong end of a hangman's rope in Genoa? That was an unpleasant thought. With no taste for sacrificial, heroic death, Theodore toyed, at Matra, with the idea of abandoning the whole project and sailing away with Captain Dick when the English brigantine appeared off the coast.

Meanwhile, in his "days of repose", telling Giafferi that he had correspondence which he must answer—letters from George II of England, from Don Carlos of Naples, from a "high person" in Versailles—Neuhoff spent many hours writing in his bare, white-washed room, while the Corsican chiefs and their "tail" of followers sat outside on the shore, watching the sea for a sight of the brigantine. He wrote[36] first to his cousin, Baron Drost, the Grand Commander of the *Deutsche Ritter* in Cologne.

My Respected Cousin,
The regard and kindness which you continually showed me, from my tenderest youth up, make me hope that you still honour me with a place in your memory and heart. Although I—on account of the derangement and confusion of my affairs caused by certain enemies, and perhaps, too, on account of my own natural inclination and desire to travel about without maintaining any communication with my former

friends, with a view, as I hoped, of being one day useful to my fellow-men—have let slip so many years without informing you of my condition; yet I pray you to believe . . . that I had had no other ambition but to return to my fatherland as soon as I could do so in a position to show my gratitude to my benefactors and friends and to crush the unjust calumnies that have been spread abroad regarding me. . . .

It has been my fortune, after many persecutions and adversities, to come personally to this Kingdom of Corsica, and to accept the offer of the faithful inhabitants here, who have elected and proclaimed me their Captain and King. For, inasmuch as I, after having for two years been at great expense on their account, and having suffered imprisonment and persecution, was no longer in a position to prosecute further travels with a view to freeing them from the tyrannous rule of the Genoese, I at last betook myself hither in accordance with their desire, and became recognized and proclaimed as their King; and I hope, by God's help, to maintain myself as such. . . .

It will not be known to you that a year ago I had the misfortune to be captured on the sea, and taken to Algiers as a slave. I was able, however, to deliver myself from bondage, having suffered, nevertheless, great loss.

NEUHOFF,
King of Corsica, by election.

In a postscript, Theodore added the hope that his friends would come and accept "such employment as they might desire and give him counsel".

In this letter, the charlatan, liar and self-pitying play-actor emerges with a clarity no apologia can disguise. In his services to the Corsicans, Neuhoff had been to no "great expense"; his "imprisonment" had been for the personal and highly discreditable affair of Jabach's loan; and he had never been "captured on the sea". The tone of the letter is such as to suggest that Theodore had in mind the probability that he might soon have to follow it up by one more of his familiar requests to his cousin for a little loan.

The same attempt to present himself as a magnanimous crusader on the Corsicans' behalf is to be seen in another letter which Neuhoff's fluent pen concocted at Matra. It was addressed to "an Irish Gentleman", and (with his permission) was published—as Theodore, I suspect, in- tended—in the *Daily Post* of London ("faithfully translated from the French") on May 8, 1736; and it was reprinted in the *Gentleman's Magazine* for that month. It ran:

Dear and Faithful Friend,

Since the year 1720, I have been seeking, all over the World, with great Pains, for a place to pass the rest of my Days with Honour, and without being obliged to be the subject of any Potentate whatsoever; to which I had a natural aversion. At last, by the Protection of the Emperor of *Morocco* and by the Assistance of the Bey of *Tunis*, I met an opportunity to offer myself to the noble Corsicans (whom I have furnished with all sorts of Ammunition and Provisions since the year 1733) who, by two of their Deputies, offered me the Sovereignty of that Island. . . .

The Offer was not displeasing to me. . . . I came here in March . . . and was received with great Demonstrations of Joy and Thankfulness. I have settled my Court, ordered six Regiments to be formed, and Macdonal,* one of your friends, takes great pains to discipline them after the *German* Manner. . . . I keep this Island at present with Ease, and am well beloved by all my subjects. In short, I think myself now happy, because I am in a Condition to make some Amends to all the Friends who have accompanied me through the World of Troubles I have passed.

* From the absence of any reference in Costa's diary to "Macdonal", the inference might be drawn that this letter was a forgery. I feel, however, that its style rings true.

(The letter ended with an invitation to the "Irish Gentleman" to come to Corsica, accept a colonel's commission, and assist the writer in "the Management of the Kingdom".)

To complete the post-bag for his courier, Neuhoff added a letter[37] for his step-father, M Marneau. It was that of a worried, rather anxious adventurer. Inviting Marneau and his family to come to Corsica and share in his good fortune, he added that he had still to "dislodge the enemy from two places—so pray for me". He went on to say that he needed two warships to blockade Bastia. He could pay for all such aid; but at present, through heavy expenses, he was a trifle "short". Here again, as in the letter to his cousin, the way for a "little loan" is clearly being prepared.

Where is certainty to be found in the reading of the mind of a man two centuries dead? Costa stayed with Paoli at Cervione; he was not at Matra to jot down the talks between Neuhoff and Giafferi, whom the baron trusted more than most of the Corsicans. Did the leathery-faced rebel chief tell Theodore bluntly that he must "go through with it", now that he was launched on an enterprise to which he (Giafferi) had given his backing? Or was Neuhoff's eventual decision to stand by his gamble motivated by the fact that, as one chronicler[38] alleges, a girl's face in Cervione had caught and held his eye? We may, I think, conclude that neither Giafferi's arguments nor the lure of a pretty Corsican girl were the decisive factor. The pupil of Görtz had smelled money, and he had nothing to lose. Screwing up his courage, he decided, after a week in Matra, to go back to Cervione.

Installed, once more, in the Bishop's Palace, Neuhoff found that matters had progressed. Paoli—his little boy, Pasquale, often at his heels—had proceeded, with Costa's aid, in organizing 216 companies, each headed by a captain; Arrighi and Fabiani (the latter with five bravely trapped horses and 100 men) had arrived. A council was held; and though Arrighi considered that the bestowal of kingship on the baron would be premature until a solid success against the Genoese had been achieved, the majority were for an immediate election.

For the business of settling the constitution and crowning the king, it was decided to move to the convent of Alesani, in a valley between Cervione and the high mountains; and there, thanks to the good offices of one Giovanni Pasquino, the Court was soon lodged "comfortably"—a point clearly of importance to Costa, whose legal talents now had full scope. After long debates, a constitution with a score of Articles was approved. The main provisions (which I summarize from a copy in the Record Office, sent home by Mr Consul Bagshaw of Genoa) were as follows:

(1) Theodore, Baron von Neuhoff, is declared Sovereign and first King of Corsica, with succession to his heirs male, by right of primogeniture, or to his female heirs, in default of male succession—provided always that the Sovereign must be of the Roman Catholic Faith,* and that, should the line become extinct, the people of Corsica shall have the right to dispose of the Kingdom.

(2) All legislative power derives from the Assembly, and is vested by the Assembly in a Diet of 24, of whom three must always reside at the King's Court, and must approve all proposals for new taxes and acts either of war or peace.

(3) Corsicans alone shall fill public offices and enjoy honours.

(4) After the expulsion of the Genoese, the King shall have the right to a personal bodyguard composed either of

---

* It is to be supposed that Theodore turned Catholic while in Spain. His family was Protestant.

Corsicans or foreigners (but *not* Genoese) and shall be permitted to maintain in Corsica foreign troops not exceeding 1,200 in number.

(5) The King is empowered to create an Order of Nobility.

(6) All property of the Genoese and of the Greek colony at Cargèse is confiscated. (The colony had been "collabora-tors.")

Other Articles fixed, *pro tem.*, the level of taxes; sanctioned stipulated weights and measures; and enjoined the king to establish and finance (in consultation with the Diet) a university for the study of law. In this final provision one detects the hand of Costa, while the Order of Nobility (of which more later) was Theodore's own idea.

By and large, it will be seen, the constitution gave the king very limited powers. The Corsicans were electing, not a dictator, but a monarch hedged about with strict constitutional safeguards. Howbeit, the "conditions", as they were called, for the coronation were now determined. On Saturday, April 14, High Mass was celebrated, followed by much noisy expenditure of powder; and on Sunday came the crowning.

First, Mass, then a speech by Giacinto Paoli; then the "showing" of Theodore on a balcony—to the accompaniment of frenzied cheers and firing of muskets. After that came a banquet in the refectory (100 covers laid, Costa much gratified), ending with toasts and impromptu poems —Paoli declaiming his compositions, glass in hand, to loud applause. Meanwhile, in the open square outside the monastery, a platform had been constructed and heaped with cut sprays of flowering cistus and arbutus from the *maquis*. On it were three chairs, the biggest in the middle. Thither Theodore was led by Paoli and Giafferi, who sat to right and left of him. A crown of chestnut twigs tied with ribbons had been made; but Fabiani declared it to be "unseemly". Hurriedly a diadem of laurel was substituted, and placed on Theodore's head. Costa made a speech; Giafferi read the constitution; the chiefs filed past the tribunal, paying homage on one knee; the crowd cheered wildly and fired muskets into the air. Then, entering the church, Theodore swore fealty to the constitution on "the Book of the Sacred Evangelists"; the chiefs swore fealty to the king; a Te Deum was sung by two choirs; and the proceedings closed with a Benediction scarcely audible through the crashes of what Costa—with obvious delight—calls "an infinite number of shots". So great was the uproar —despite the Corsicans' shortage of powder—that the commandant of San Pellegrino felt constrained to send another *felucca* to Bastia. Something *must* be afoot!

Monday morning—as might be expected after the "quiet but lengthy supper" which rounded off Coronation Day—found King Theodore a little tired. Following an example he had learned from Philip V in Madrid, he "received" while lying in bed. From that easeful position he announced the appointment of Paoli and Giafferi as Joint First Ministers and Commanders-in-Chief. Giappiconi was made Secretary for War; Costa, Grand Chancellor, Secretary of State and Keeper of the Seals. To Xaviero di Matra, ennobled as Marquis, fell the appointment of Grand Marshal, to Arrighi the post of Inspector General of the Army. Dr Gaffori became Cabinet Secretary and Marquis. Cups of chocolate were handed round—as if it were Versailles, not a remote village in the savage Corsican hills —while the King created counts and marquises with grace and generosity.

Too great a generosity, thought Paoli and Giafferi. Observing, on the outer door of the house, a list, affixed by Costa, of these new patents of nobility, the two generals for once saw eye to eye. They wrenched the paper off the door and tore it contemptuously to shreds. Costa appeased the angry king by re-writing the list and replacing it on the door; but more hard words were to follow. Learning that Theo-dore had appointed Fabiani as Vice-President of the War Council, Paoli complained that this infringed his authority; and only with difficulty was he persuaded to renounce his threat to abandon the king and return to his mountains.

It was against this background of jealousies and feuds that the Court, on April 17, moved back to Cervione. It was, says Costa, a triumphal progress. In every village there were garlanded windows and decorated arches; the prin-cipal families were "presented"; and the streets were lined with men who doffed their caps and women who curtsied. At a monastery where the cortège halted, the monks brought offerings of wine and fruit; and, on the king's gracious refusal of the gifts, they joined the happy procession and distributed their presents to the poor they passed. On the king's arrival at the Bishop's Palace, the cheering throng was so thick that two captains had to be stationed—one in the porch, one within—to keep order. Costa, I fear, was exaggerating the numbers of the population, if not the enthusiasm; but, metaphorically, it was, no doubt, "roses, roses all the way". Theodore felt, that day, that Ripperdà would be proud of him. Uneasy memories of jail in Leg-horn, scurvy months spent in hiding from exorbitant creditors, faded from his mind: adventure paid dividends.

The cheering over, he soon found sterner tasks to face: bad news came from the coast. Captain Dick had duly reached Leghorn and begun negotiations for some more munitions and the promised royal robes. He ran into trouble. The Genoese had already lodged protests with all the powers at the landing of this "sponsored imposter"; and Mr Fane, the British Envoy to the Court of Tuscany, heavily "pressured" by the Genoese consul at Leghorn, sent for Dick and admonished him not to return to Corsica. Dick, who claimed—quite falsely—that Theodore had "a letter" from George II, ignored the warning and set sail for Corsica with such cargo as he had managed to secure. (Fane had to rest content with instructing the British consul to impound Dick's passport, if he returned, and to advise the port authorities of Leghorn not to give his ship clearance.) On Dick's arrival at Corsica, however, ill luck befell. Fabiani had been instructed to meet the ship at Prunete—where landing had to be by boat on the beach— and to accept delivery of the cargo. When twelve bags of bullets and six barrels of powder had been got ashore, a furious dispute arose among the Corsicans as to their apportionment.

This wasted precious time. While the ship's boat was making another trip to shore—carrying the famous robes, three cases of muskets and six Corsicans—a Genoese *felucca* slipped up and captured boat, passengers, cargo and crew of Devon sailors, who were taken to Bastia[39] and kept in jail until the efforts of the British vice-consul secured their release. When this sorry news reached Cervione, the king, says Costa, was "sad at heart, but showed no outward signs of chagrin". He must, however, have realized that these faction-feuds would prove the undoing of the whole enterprise unless Corsican passions could be diverted against the enemy.

Accordingly, the organization of the Resistance was pressed forward. A flag was designed—green and yellow, with "*In Te, Domine, speravi*" as device; and the Kingdom's Arms were decreed—a Moor's head with three links of broken chain. This conceit, thought Theodore, nicely harmonized past and present—the liberation of Corsica from the Saracens by Count Boniface in 930 and his own liberating crusade, with its starting-point in Africa.

Twenty-four captains were appointed, each to command 300 men; and decrees were circularized throughout the districts of Ampugnani and Casacconi, ordering every armed man to report for duty with victuals for four days. Attention was paid also to what we should now call "psychological warfare". On April 19, Costa signed a proclamation designed to show the king's "clemency and paternal love". An amnesty was offered to all "collaborators" who made submission within ten days; after that their property would be confiscated and "severe punishment" meted out to their persons, on apprehension.

The next step was to move the Court from Cervione to Venzolasca, a village better placed for operations against the nervous Genoese commandant of the fort of San Pellegrino. Once again Costa has to record dissensions among the chiefs. The quarters selected for the king at Venzolasca consisted of a house in which the first floor, the *piano nobile*, had four rooms—the guards and servants sleeping below. The best room was naturally set aside for Theodore; Giafferi and Giappiconi were allotted a room each; and the fourth room was shared by Costa and the Sicilian, Buongiorno. This meant that Paoli, who had had priority in the quartering at Cervione, must now lodge with the chief captains in a neighbouring house. He did not conceal his high dudgeon; and his followers from Moro-saglia and Rostino began to stage a mutinous riot, shouting: "Our General should have been crowned!" Striding forth from his quarters with appropriate sense of the dramatic, Theodore laid about him with his famous cane, and ordered the guards to seize, and drag into the house, the seeming ring-leader, one Capone, on whom the king passed sum-mary sentence of death for mutiny.

The riot swelled: Capone's friends called for brushwood to burn the royal quarters and all the inmates. Paoli burst into the king's chamber and threatened to throw Theodore through the window. It took all the efforts of Costa and the others to restore peace—at a price which scarcely enhanced the royal authority. Capone was pardoned; Giafferi and Giappiconi agreed to "double-up"; Paoli got his room. Supper, relates Costa, was amicable: Theodore's cook did his best with the tough meat of Corsica to restore lost tempers.

It was plain, however, that no more time must be lost in starting military operations—even with the limited resources now available. The plan adopted was to make the main effort in the north. Paoli, with the bulk of the insurgents' force, was to invest and endeavour to storm Bastia. Fabiani was to raise fresh troops in his own district, the Balagne, and try to seize Calvi by surprise. Arrighi was to assault St Florent and Nebbio, at the base of Cap Corse. Theodore himself would "direct", with less personal risk, the operations against San Pellegrino; he would have Captain Ortoli as his field commander. Giafferi, Giappiconi and Costa would remain at the Venzolasca headquarters, while a small force under Luccioni—a chief who makes a brief and tragic appearance at this stage—would move south against Porto-Vecchio and Bonifacio, where there were believed to be numerous "collaborators" who must be persuaded to see the error of their unpatriotic ways. As for the wild west coast, Costa has nothing to say; but Mr Robinson at the British Embassy in Vienna received about this time a report[40] from Leghorn that "all that part of the island on the other side of the mountains has submitted" to the "unknown person".

The London *Daily Post* of May 11 printed a dispatch from its Bastia correspondent (clearly a Genoese) bewailing the wealth of the insurrection. "The money rolling among them is Sequins, Mirlitons, French Louis, Moidores,

Lisbonnes and other Pieces of Gold." There was little truth in the story, nor can we accept the *Post's* judgment, in its next issue, that the Corsicans "seem very much in love with their new Government, because it ushers in, with the rest, a plenty of Gold". There had been much more silver than gold in the casks disembarked at Aleria; and Paoli's cash bonuses for volunteers were already a heavy drain. The king was full of promises: ample funds from abroad were on the way. But, as Secretary Gaffori was well aware, the Treasury was in no sense "rolling in money".

All the same, it is evident that Theodore, despite his troubles with the warring chiefs, still felt that bluff might succeed. On April 26 he wrote to a friend in Paris, sug-gesting *inter alia* that Louis XV might be asked to receive an accredited envoy from the King of Corsica at his Court. Effrontery reached its peak. He made Costa a marquis, and ennobled many captains as "Hereditary Knights of the Golden Key". In an address from the throne to his followers at this period, he declared that "Princes are like living laws and shining mirrors; by looking closely into them, subjects may learn to imitate them." The actor still took comfort in the footlights.

CHAPTER SEVEN

The Crumbling of the Throne

THE insurgents' campaign, as Theodore had indeed fore-
seen, was handicapped from the start by the weakness of
their armoury. Paoli drove in the Genoese posts round
Bastia, seized Furiani and other neighbouring villages, and
captured the outlying strong-point of St Joseph. In the
town, which held apparently a number of sympathizers
with the rebel cause, rumour and alarm ran wild. Theodore,
it was said, had undertaken to unfurl the flag of Spain (or of
Don Carlos of Naples) over the first important place which
fell into his hands: the insurgents were set on bloody
massacre. Signor D'Angelo, the French vice-consul,
wrote[41] anxiously to M Campredon, Louis XV's Envoy
at Genoa: "The Corsicans boast that if they get into Bastia,
they will spit us like fowls for roasting. God save us from
such a fate!"

No hero (one would judge), the poor vice-consul need
not have worried: there was a Genoese garrison of 4,000
men, the walls of Bastia were thick, and Paoli had little or
no ammunition for such of the ten cannon as were allotted
to him. An attempt by the rebels to storm the small Fort des
Capucins at the main gateway into Bastia was repulsed
with loss, and a surprise night assault on the town ended in

failure and confusion. On the eve of the attack, Paoli received news that his old father was on his death-bed at Orezza; heedless of the consequences, he rode homewards instantly, leaving his troops leaderless. Bastia had little more to fear from its besiegers.

When the news of this reverse, and its cause, reached Venzolasca, the king—in a burst of real temper which needed no play-acting—was for having Paoli court martialled and condemned to death for betraying his trust and leaving the field in defiance of orders. Giafferi, however, took a more lenient view, despite his personal jealousy of Paoli. Characteristically he resented a "foreigner's" demand for the punishment of a Corsican chief: it was "the tradition of Corsica," he told Theodore, "that every respect should be paid to the dying and the dead". At all events, there was no court martial, though the king sulked for a whole day and once more threatened, with becomingly dramatic gestures, to leave the island to its fate.

Worse news, however, was soon to come. While Theodore was engaged in making his dispositions for an attack on San Pellegrino, a loyal partisan arrived hot-foot from the south. Luccioni had changed sides: having captured Sartène and Porto-Vecchio, he had sold the latter town back to the Genoese for 30 *zecchini*.* For good measure he had included in the bargain a complete disclosure of the rebels' plan of campaign, and he was now plotting a still blacker treachery: he was on his way to see Theodore and persuade him to come to the south, where a trap was laid for the king's betrayal into Genoese hands.

Sure enough, next afternoon, Luccioni arrived—hiding perfidy behind a bold front. This time Theodore decided

---

* The figure is Costa's, and I incline to the suspicion that the lawyer had read his Scripture and put down what he regarded, no doubt, as *le numéro juste*.

that his role as "monarch" demanded a display of kingly resolution. Denouncing Luccioni in the presence of Giafferi, Giappiconi, Costa and such captains as were present, the king gave the traitor until sunset to say his prayers. The Court, says Costa, proceeded meanwhile to table "in sombre mood"—as well it might. Giafferi and Giappiconi urged a reprieve; Costa rose, glass in hand, crying: "Long live the King! Let justice triumph and clemency prevail!" Neither Giafferi's pleas for prudence nor Costa's endeavour to get the best of both worlds had any effect on the king, who sat silent, "white-faced, but calm and inexorable". Supper ended, a sullen firing-squad obeyed Theodore's commands. Luccioni, stark in the dust, was dead: a vendetta was born.

That night the king slept uneasily and woke, in the grey dawn, wondering if he had acted wisely. Life was cheap in Corsica; but Giafferi's face had been grim. The play-actor had stepped out of his pantomime role: he had a man's blood on his hands. An error, perhaps. Theodore pondered long: if he were to "get away" with this exercise in royal severity, he must "build himself up" all the more as kingly. On with the motley! One eighteenth-century chronicler[42] records how, at this time Theodore indulged to the full his bent for histrionics: when he was not gazing seawards from a vantage point to descry the sails of succouring ships whose arrival was "daily imminent", he would closet himself in his quarters writing dispatches to "other kings of his acquaintance" on the mainland. He even contrived—Buongiorno helped here—the frequent arrival of sealed missives which reached him impressively from his friendly royal correspondents! What Costa and Giafferi thought about all this is not recorded.

Costa was busily and (one imagines) happily engaged in the congenial task of drafting a lengthy and (truth to tell)

Left: THEODORE LANDS IN MOTLEY. From *Histoire des Révolutions de l'Ile de Corse,* 1738
Right: THE "KING ON STILTS". From *De Gekroonde Moff,* The Hague, 1738

DECORATION: THE MOOR'S HEAD
From *Giustificazione delle Rivoluzione di Corsica,* 1764

THEODORE

VIEW OF GAETA

Taken from the Life, (by Order of his Neapolitan Majesty) while under Confinement in the Castle of Gaeta.

KING THEODORE IN PRISON AT GAETA
From an Engraving in the British Museum

rather tedious manifesto[43] in rejoinder to current Genoese denunciations of "an imposter dyed dark with dabbling in the Kabbala and black arts". But the king was ill at ease at Venzolasca: there were too many frowning faces. In its issue of June 5, the *Daily Post* published the translation of a further letter written by Theodore to his friend "the Irish gentleman". Answering, apparently, a letter from Ireland, the king said he agreed it might be prudent not to come to Corsica "until the whole island is entirely subdued to my obedience". The letter went on to recount how eight Corsicans had had to be executed for treason. "This was the more reluctant to me . . . for, though Power may compel Bodies, it can never conquer Inclination. And anything that carries the Face of Cruelty along with it . . . must needs estrange the Minds of Men." This letter, for all its insincerity and pretension of noble sentiments, was penned by a worried man. Towards the end of May, Theodore went north to join Fabiani in the Balagne.

Once again as in the case of the visit to Matra before the Coronation, Costa has nothing to record in his diary about the motives which induced Theodore to leave his headquarters. Cynics, of course, may say that Fabiani, whose "bravely trapped horses" Costa had admired when the Balagne chieftain joined the Court, was a relatively well-to-do Corsican: he would be a good host, and the wine of the district is renowned. But the king had more substantial reasons for his departure. The undisguised resentment of Giafferi and Arrighi at the execution of Luccioni was bad enough: their warnings that he must expect a vendetta from Luccioni's clan preyed on Theodore's nerves. But the incident which finally decided him to go north was much less creditable than the summary execution of a traitor. Forgetting his regal part, the king had scandalized his audience.

7

"Princes are like living laws and shining mirrors"? This was all very well for a public address to an impressionable crowd of mountaineers; but even a prince, thought Theodore, must have a gentleman's distractions from the dull affairs of State. So he did more than cast an eye at the young woman whose face had caught his attention at Cervione. She was the sister[44] of a member of Theodore's bodyguard; and in the heat of a late afternoon the king suggested to her that his room was an interesting place for what Scots lairds of those days called "houghmagandie". Apprised of his sister's danger, the brother burst into Theodore's chamber—just in time to save her from a fate worse, in Corsican eyes, than death.

The signal for supper and Costa's polite entry saved the situation for the moment; but, during the meal, the king heard the sound of blows and weeping. What was it? The brother was teaching his sister to repent unchastity. In royal (if not wholly righteous) wrath, Theodore shouted "*lèse-majesté*", summoned the young man, and would have had him hanged by the neck out of the window when he "spoke back" truculently and menaced the king with a brandished chair. The ministers and generals took a different view: virginity in Corsica was not lightly to be taken even by royalty; and the king would be well advised to watch his step. The episode was discreetly omitted by Costa from his diary; but, then, the Keeper of the Seals was an *aficionado* of the king. Less enthusiastically loyal, Giafferi told the king bluntly that, if he must go "leaping into bed", it had better be with a mistress imported from the mainland. The king saw the point, and sent an invitation to a Mlle Champigny, a young Frenchwoman of his acquaintance in Nice: she would enjoy, he wrote, a visit to his romantic kingdom. Meanwhile, to let the scandal blow over, Theodore left tactfully for "an inspection" of Fabiani's forces. Costa was given, so he says, "vice-regal" authority to carry on in the king's absence.

Poor Costa! That summer found him beset with manifold troubles. Above all, the stock of *zecchini* brought from Tunis was long since exhausted (a factor, no doubt, in Luccioni's treachery); and though Marquis Xaviero di Matra, the Grand Marshal, tried hard to raise funds by appeals through the clergy and perquisitions by a captain in his district, the villages had "neither gold, silver nor even copper". So, with the approval presumably of the Diet's delegates, a bold decision was taken: a new coinage should be struck. From Rostino, at Costa's invitation, came Don Matteo d'Ortiporio, a priest who had a reputation as a skilful forger of Genoese money— "and not ashamed to own his repute". To aid this adroit cleric at the Mint, which was to be set up in a monastery in the village of Tavagna, Costa sent for a team of smiths headed by Giulio Francesco of Orezza, a craftsman so cunning that he was known as "Seven Brains". Pietro Gaffori (the Cabinet Secretary) was elected President of the Mint, and enjoined to collect metal for the coinage.

That, of course, was the difficulty. Silver was not to be had. Don Matteo devised the mould for a noble silver piece, which was to have the value of 3 *livres*. On the obverse were the Arms of the Kingdom—the Moor's head supporting a closed crown, and three links of broken chain. On the reverse was the figure of the Virgin Mary, with five stars, and the legend: *Monstra Te esse Matrem*. So far as is known, only one silver piece was ever struck. The Mint had to do its best with brass (the convent at Corte contributed some crucifixes and braziers), and confined itself to the production of humble 5 *soldi* and 2½ *soldi* pieces. Writing two years later, Jaussin (the naval doctor) complains that, even then, those coins were sadly defaced. The specimens that have survived show faintly, on the obverse, *Theodorus D.G. unanimo consensu electus Rex et Princeps Regni Corsici*; and, on the reverse, a crown sup/ported by palms, with the legend: *Pro Bono Publico Re Co.* Centred were the letters T. R., which, the Genoese said, stood for *Tutti Rebelli*, and the Corsicans for *Tutto Rame* (all copper). The coins quickly became collectors' pieces on the mainland,[45] but they were misliked in the island. Costa sadly records that, though a salutary effect resulted from the jailing, at the king's orders, of two women who refused this "legal tender", it was never possible to get the new money accepted in Orezza, the one market available to rebel H.Q. for salt, shoes and cloth. "This," he com/ments tersely, "was very inconvenient."

Costa's correspondence at this time with the king, during the Royal sojourn in the Balagne, is illuminating. One discerns a worried little man—less fleshy, one imagines, now that the stores of wine and "delicious dates" from Tunis had run out—burdened by his "vice/regal" responsibilities. On June 8, he writes, there was a disap/pointment: five ships had been sighted, but had sailed on towards Sardinia. (The story,[46] current in England after/wards, that Theodore's nephew, the young Comte de Trévoux, now landed with ten cannon and 30,000 *louis d'or* is certainly untrue.) Count Poggi of Ziccavo, added Costa, had sent some cheese (of goat's milk, one fears) and had promised 100 men. But would they come? Meanwhile there were desertions: it was harvest/time and men were going off to their holdings* without leave. Discipline was deteriorating, and there were no mules to get the cannon

---

* One catches here an unmistakable echo of Jacobite tribulations in the Highlands of Scotland. Costa has a harsh name for these deserters: "Vittoli," he calls them fiercely, after the name of Sampiero's assassin. But they had wives and children, and a lost harvest would mean starvation.

into firing positions against San Pellegrino. When would the king return?

A week later Costa renews his plea that the king should rejoin his H.Q. The Genoese morale in San Pellegrino, he wrote, was low: deserters were coming over by night to the insurgents with their arms. But, without more powder and shot, he (Costa) could do nothing, and the king's absence was leading to defeatist talk: "the foreigner had taken all Corsica's money and was about to fly to France". The finances of the Resistance were becoming desperate, and 140 *pistoles* (about £100) for pay of the troops had had to be found "out of my own pocket, which is now empty". (Odd gloss on newspaper accuracy is the report, a few weeks earlier, in the London *Daily Journal*, that Theodore was paying his army every three days, "which gives them such life that no town can withstand them".)

By the end of June, things had got so difficult that the Grand Chancellor sent Christoforo Buongiorno to Theodore with a further message. Gaffori was making a hash of his minting; he kept complaining of the cunning ill-will (*la malignité rusée*) of the smiths, and wanted to have the whole team clapped in jail; but in fact the President of the Mint was a "pleasure girl (*une fille*): one day's work and he's tired of it all". As for Buongiorno himself, this genial Sicilian was too amenable to flattery: he would lavish munitions from the scanty store on those who cozened him, not realizing that there were "robbers" in Corsica. And who knew, asked Costa, in real personal distress, what Buongiorno was doing with the food supplies? One surmises that the H.Q. mess was getting Spartan fare.

Uncomfortable news, all this, for Theodore in the Balagne. But worse tidings followed fast. First, ominous news of the defection of the Marquis Xaviero di Matra, who went off to his village with his "tail"; then the receipt by Costa of an alarming letter from a young nephew in the south: the family of Luccioni were swearing vengeance, and something like a counter-revolution was being organized by one Luca, who was claiming the throne for himself and calling Theodore rude names.*

Even so, the king at this stage was not disposed to abandon his enterprise: the gamble, with luck, might still be won. Taking up a position at Monte Maggiore, near Calenzana —a little town lying between Calvi and the mountains—he wrote urgently to Paoli for reinforcements. They did not come: Paoli—jealous of Fabiani—replied that there were "harvest difficulties"; but with the limited forces at his disposal, Theodore launched, undismayed, a heavy attack on Calenzana. For lack of powder and shot, the assault failed, but the king showed himself, on this occasion— wrote the admiring Costa—a good tactician and "a man of courage". For once, let us say, the play-actor faced real powder and shot.

This was not the only reverse. At about the same time, the Genoese captain, Bembo, who was holding Algajola— a little town in the Balagne—with 300 men, made a successful sortie against the rebels: he captured some prisoners and a cannon, duly sent to Bastia "with great pomp". Governor Rivarola had a thankful Te Deum sung. He had, it appears, other grounds for thankfulness: according to Costa, Arrighi—now conducting, with less than a hundred ill-armed men, desultory operations against Bastia—was in treasonable touch with the Genoese.

Theodore fell ill; or possibly he feigned illness, as he later (we shall see) feigned gout. Issuing from the Balagne a

* "*Teodoro è Re de' coglioni*"—a phrase to be found in the works of Mr Hemingway.

plaintive proclamation declaring that the whole population of Corsica could not be counts or generals, he
wrote to Costa with two urgent requests: first, the Grand
Chancellor must send him at once a bodyguard of forty
"safe men"; secondly, he must hoist on the tower of Paduella,
near San Pellegrino, a parti-coloured flag to guide the
expected munition ships. (None, of course, were "expected":
once more Theodore was lying, or at least whistling, to
keep up others' courage.)

Recovered from his distemper—real or diplomatic—the
king left the Balagne. The route led towards Corte. When
they neared the island's old fortified city, Giappiconi,
Arrighi and others deserted their royal leader. Sending an
urgent message for help to Costa ("failing that, Corsica
will earn obloquy for murdering in cold blood her King
and Father"), Theodore waited in the *maquis* between
Ponte Lecchia and Corte until Gaffori (dispatched by
Costa) arrived with a loyal band. Lodged for a night in
the nearby monastery of St Francis, Theodore tried to enter
the town of Corte. Arrighi, who had "gone underground"
in the town, barred the way: there were hard words, shots,
and dead on each side. In the skirmish, one Schietto, in the
king's party, set fire to the town, burning thirty-six houses.
According to a report published in the *Mercure de France*
(September) and reprinted a month later in the *Gentleman's Magazine*, Arrighi's mother and three other relations
perished in one house thus destroyed. The facts about this
holocaust are obscure; but the "royalists" had clearly the
better of it; Arrighi fled "over the mountains"; Corte made
homage to the king; and, surprisingly, Paoli appeared once
more on the scene, with renewed professions of loyalty.

Encouraged by this, Theodore, decided that he would
rejoin his forces on the east coast. Informed of this decision,
Costa relates that he busied himself preparing the Franciscan

monastery near Venzolasca as a royal residence. He summoned workmen and

> ... a painter from Ampugnani to paint the arms of the King
> and of the kingdom, all surrounded by flowers in arabesque,
> before the door of each room. I hung portières of silks of
> various hues, and I adorned the royal bed with silk hangings.
> ... The Court appeared as if made with flowers ... to
> conceal the poverty which lay behind it.

According to Varnhagen, who was one of Theodore's
most sentimental German biographers, "several ships" with
munitions arrived at this period. There is no evidence to
support this statement; nor is there any more substance in
Signor D'Angelo's view, in his letters [47] during the summer,
that "the rebels are solidly united". Indeed the *Daily
Journal*, in its reports from Leghorn, carried the facts:
Theodore was now writing to Naples, asking (vainly) for
the "protection" of Don Carlos. No reinforcements of arms
came from Tunis or Italy; and the dissensions among the
chieftains grew more and more bitter.

Genoese agents, meanwhile, had been sedulously inciting
the Luccioni family to take their revenge. Their chosen
victim, although he had not been present at Luccioni's
execution, was Simon Fabiani. It was a wantonly cruel
choice; for there is evidence that [48] Fabiani had played some
part in "reconciling" Theodore and the Luccionis, among
whose clan the king had hopefully distributed titles. On
July 13 Fabiani went to Orezza, where his wife's family
lived, to await the "hundred men" promised, as we have
seen, by Count Poggi. Next day he made a trip to Stazzone
(between Orezza and Cervione), and there fell in with a
group of Luccioni partisans, whom he entertained at
supper. The following morning he was ambushed by them
and shot: lying by the road, he forbade his small escort to

pursue the assassins lest they elude pursuit and return, to cut off their victim's head.[49] Carried back to Stazzone, Fabiani of the "bravely trapped horses" died that night in agony.

That was a sad blow for Theodore: the Genoese from Bastia began making successful sorties; and a magniloquent appeal[50] issued by Canon Orticoni for "patriotism and unity" did little to heal the feuds. Tantalizingly, fortune gave the king, at this point, some small successes. A Corsican priest, Salvini, landed near Ile Rousse with twenty-two barrels of powder, seventeen bags of bullets and some guns—all bought, apparently, on credit in Leghorn. Thus reinforced, the patriots in the Balagne routed a Genoese seaborne "commando" under Colonel Marchelli, who landed to attack a rebel tower; and in the panic-stricken flight to their ship, lying off-shore, many Genoese were drowned and 130 taken prisoner. In the same week, an insurgent band led by Luc Ornano lured a Genoese force from the Ajaccio garrison into an ambush, and killed 300 of them. Once again, Bastia was alarmed: Signor D'Angelo reported to Campredon that Theodore was "much reinforced", and that he had received "8,000 gold Piastres from Rome".

Alas! There was no substance in these reports; no aid from foreign powers was reaching Neuhoff. On the contrary, George II had issued, in June, an imperative warning[51] to British subjects not to aid King Theodore—a warning whose terror drove poor Captain Dick (rather unnecessarily, one feels) to suicide[52] in Smyrna. The French Government, too, was being subjected to protests from Genoa. Signor Sorba (a Corsican by birth), the Genoese Envoy in Paris, had been complaining that a relation of Theodore's, Captain Nayssen of the Regiment de La Marck, had written a letter (intercepted) offering to join the king (an accusation which Nayssen indignantly denied), and that young Trévoux (Elizabeth von Neuhoff's son) was still planning* to go with arms to Corsica.

Campredon's dispatches at this time are also full of stories of help arriving for Theodore—30,000 piastres from Tunis through the Leghorn branch of the bank of Huigens of Cologne; gold and "Arab letters" captured on a con-verted ex-Moslem monk apprehended at Sestri di Levante. French "agents" had lively imaginations. Actually, the throne was crumbling: arms and money were utterly lack-ing, and by the end of July it had become apparent to Theodore that his Corsican supporters, except for the faith-ful Costa, were already disillusioned. In its issue of August 1736, the *Mercure de Hollande* was reporting that "*la discorde a commencé à se mettre parmi eux*": Aitelli, Raffaeli and Paoli were now regarded as leaders of a faction called "the Indifferents", and the loyalty even of Luc Ornani was suspect. Theodore gloomed and cursed: even Mlle Champigny, now arrived on her romantic visit, was scant consolation.

---

* This story got a wide circulation; indeed the *Gentleman's Magazine* of October 1736 published a categoric statement that he had landed. The report had no substance.

CHAPTER EIGHT

The Flight of the Monarch

AUGUST was passed by the Court unhappily, despite Costa's decorations in the Franciscan monastery. The Genoese, though they had recruited a "Corsican Legion" of 1,500 ex-galley-slaves who committed savage atrocities in the island, were in no position to issue from their garrison towns in strength, or to deal with the insurgents in the hills. On the other hand, it was impossible for Theodore's adherents to make any impression on fortified places. Giafferi and Aitelli now seem to have been in a bitter, rebellious mood against their elected sovereign; and in the first week of September the king decided to go with Costa to Sartène—the only town of any size which he could call his own since Luccioni's "re-sale" of Porto-Vecchio. If the bid for a throne were failing, something perhaps could be retrieved from the wreckage.

Costa did not enjoy the journey. He does not describe the route in detail; but, in order (one imagines) to avoid Porto-Vecchio, he records that they "crossed the mountains" —presumably by the pass between Monte Renoso and the Incudine. (See the sketch-map over the page.) Camping each night, the king was sleepless: on his pallet of dry ferns he would engage the Grand Chancellor in talk, hour after hour, holding his scarlet caftan tight round him for warmth. In the mountains a violent thunderstorm broke and soaked them to the skin. At one village they were hospitably entertained in the house of the leading man, Giudicelli by name, to whom the king generously promised exemption from all future taxes, and a title—to be bestowed in due course. But the march was arduous, provisions were scanty. It was a tired and hungry Grand Chancellor who records thankfully in his diary that the welcome at Sartène was friendly.

Housed there in some state, thanks to the hospitality of one Micaele Durazzo, Theodore indulged in his crowning piece of regal pantomime. On September 16 he announced the establishment of an Order of Liberation, for which he promised promptly to secure Papal recognition. There would be two ranks—Illustrious Knights, and Excellent Commanders—and membership would be open, at the royal pleasure, to both Corsicans and foreigners, regardless of their religion. The ceremonial dress of the Order would be a sky-blue tunic, on which would be worn a cross and a large star of gold and enamel bearing the effigy of Justice. From one hand of Justice would hang scales, with a triangle enclosing the letter T, dependent; in the other hand Justice would hold a sword—the plaque being completed by a globe at Justice's feet, and the Kingdom's arms in one corner. Except on ceremonial occasions, the badge of Knights and Commanders would be a green ribbon.

Membership of the Order conveyed certain substantial privileges—exemption from all taxes in Corsica, immunity from prosecution for any crime other than *lèse-majesté*—and the king enacted that none save a member of the Order might henceforth command a royal ship or fort. But there were also obligations. Each member must swear to serve the king faithfully to the death, and to provide two soldiers for

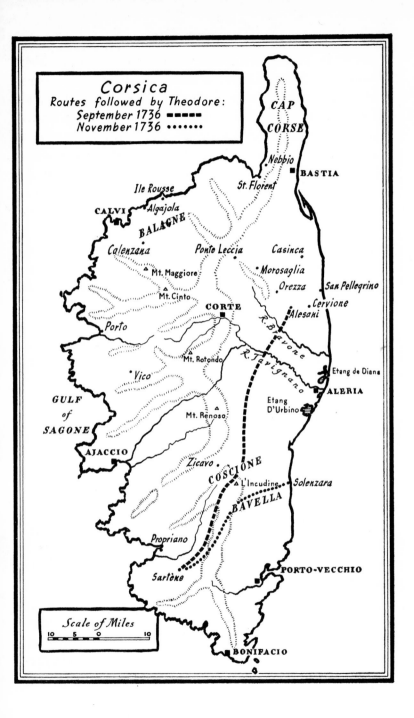

Corsica
Routes followed by Theodore:
September 1736 ▬▬▬▬
November 1736 ••••••

CAP
CORSE

Nebbio
BASTIA

Ile Rousse
St. Florent

CALVI
Algajola
BALAGNE

Calenzana
Ponte Leccia
Casinca

Mt. Maggiore
Morosaglia
Orezza
San Pellegrino

Mt. Cinto
CORTE
Alesani
Cervione

Porto
R. Brevone

Mt. Rotondo
R. Tavignano

Vico
Etang de Diana

GULF
of
SAGONE
Mt. Renoso
Etang
D'Urbino
ALERIA

AJACCIO

Zicavo
COSCIONE
L'Incudine
Solenzara

BAVELLA

Propriano

Sartène
PORTO-VECCHIO

Scale of Miles
10   5   0   10

BONIFACIO

his Majesty's service; he must always carry a sword, which would be held unsheathed at Mass; and he must recite daily Psalms XL and LXX—*Deus Noster Refugium*, and *In Te, Domine, speravi*. More material to Theodore's purposes was the rule that members must pay an entry fee of 1,000 *scudi* (almost £200). This investment would bear interest at the rate of 10 per cent!

According to one admiring biographer,[53] there was a rush to join the Order, which soon had 400 members. There were certainly not 400,000 *scudi* forthcoming in the whole of Corsica that autumn—to say nothing of sky-blue tunics and gold and enamel stars. Indeed this same historian concluded cautiously that "probably only foreigners paid the entry money". What foreigners? Buongiorno? He had prudently left the island in search of supplies, and was back in Tunis. To hearten his host, Durazzo, in Sartène, the king gave it out that his "nephew" had just arrived from Westphalia with a "cargo of arms" destined for a contingent of troops which Bonneval—would you believe it?—was sending from Albania (of all places!). No such succour was, in fact, forthcoming: everything points to Theodore's extreme isolation in the little town of Sartène.

His State activities, over which Costa, the jurist, enjoyed himself, now became legislative rather than military. Edicts issued from the palace enacting penalties for *vendetta* killings, prescribing liberty of conscience for all subjects, legalizing the manufacture of salt—hitherto a Genoese monopoly. According to one contemporary record,[54] Theodore must be credited at this stage with an almost Leninist plan for curing Corsica's economic troubles by a programme of industrialization—factories, salt pans and so forth. More play-acting! The king had shot his bolt: by the end of October the inhabitants of Sartène were obviously tired of their expensive guest; a shot fired at Theodore narrowly missed him; and on November 4—by which time there were reports that the Genoese commandant in Ajaccio was planning a raid against Sartène—a royal proclamation[55] was issued, appointing a Regency Council of twenty-eight, headed by Paoli, Giafferi and Luc Ornano. Promising gratitude and favours to all who remained faithful to him in his absence, the king would proceed to the mainland, "thereby to obtain more expeditiously succour for our cause".

Once more poor Costa has to record a terrible journey. It was decided that the king should seek embarkation at Solenzara on the east coast, mid-way between Porto-Vecchio and Aleria. Crossing the mountains near Zonza, the party suffered from the extreme cold; the only shelter at night was, now and then, an empty shepherd's hut, and their provisions were bread, a little cheese and *broccio* (curdled milk). Making their way through the Forest of Bavella, the king and his few followers had one bit of luck. At the little village of Solaro, the peasants—at first terrified—discovered Theodore's identity and killed a sheep. There was a supper—"pastoral but welcome", writes Costa—of roast mutton, followed by improvised songs. On the fifth day, Solenzara was reached, passage was secured on a small French ship trading from St Tropez (Décugis, master), and, after regal farewells, the course was set for Leghorn. Not without incident: a Genoese *felucca* hove in sight, but respected the French flag which Décugis was quick to hoist.

Towards dusk on November 14 the party—consisting[56] of the king (disguised as a priest), Sebastiano Costa and his son Giuseppe, Poggi, Durazzo di Forrani, Colonna, and some others, including a Florentine secretary, Francesco dell' Agata—stepped ashore at Leghorn. Décugis was "carpeted" by the French consul and kept for a short time under arrest. The fugitives discreetly vanished. The Dutch Press reported that the king had gone to Albano, in order to offer his throne to "James III"; and the *Daily Journal* had it that he had left Corsica, "not owing to any straits he was reduced to, but to some important affairs he has to transact in Italy, for facilitating the conquest of Corsica". Theodore had indeed already begun to concoct plans for making capital even out of defeat; but these needed time to mature. He went, first, to Pescia, near Lucca, then to Florence.

His presence there soon became known to Viale, the Genoese Envoy, who demanded that the Tuscan authorities arrest him. But though Viale offered a reward of 100 *pistoles* (£85) for Theodore's apprehension, all that the Florentine police did was to arrest the king's confessor.[57] It seems likely that the authorities were not over-zealous in the matter (Genoa was unpopular in Florence), and the wary Theodore never slept twice in the same bed. By day he wrote letters indefatigably—appealing for aid and hinting (in one letter intercepted by the Genoese) that he had George II's support in his enterprise.

Eventually, through the good offices of one Baglioni, a *valet de chambre* at the Court, he secured[58] an interview with Grand Duke Gian Gastone, the last of the ruling Medicis. Possibly because that elderly rake had a German wife, he treated the Westphalian adventurer generously: "lending" him 100 *zecchini* (£45), "as one ruling Prince to another", he promised to protect Theodore—adding that it would be wise to send the Corsicans packing. This advice the king followed, and most of his party went back to Corsica. Early in December, Canon Orticoni, accompanied by Forrani and Colonna, sailed from Leghorn and landed at Poragiola in the Balagne.

This voyage caused the watchful M Campredon in Genoa to prick up his ears. Orticoni had recently been appointed almoner to Don Carlos, King of the Two Sicilies; and the ship on which he crossed to Corsica belonged to the Spanish consul at Leghorn. What a ploy! For years Campredon had tried to persuade his masters in Paris that France ought to own Corsica. Now he wrote,[59] in an "I told you so" mood, that if he could secure a port in Corsica, Orticoni's arrangement was to offer the island to Don Carlos—who "might not refuse it".

Whether Orticoni could then have persuaded the Corsicans to accept this solution is doubtful: the "ultra-nationalists" were always opposed to foreign aid. But Genoa must be shown that the "kingdom" of Corsica would fight on for independence. Shortly after the canon's arrival in the island, the three Chief Regents issued a manifesto[60] in Theodore's favour:

> We declare before Almighty God, who sees into our hearts and knows the justice of our cause, and before the whole world that H.M. King Theodore I, since the day he arrived in Corsica, worked only for the happiness of this illustrious nation, and left Corsica only to secure means to set the seal on our well-being. We remain his faithful and loving subjects.

An agreeable testimonial, one would say; but the Regents never really expected to see their monarch again. Flattering words cost nothing, and the Senate in Genoa might be impressed by this "loyal" defiance.

Meanwhile Florence was becoming unhealthy for Theodore in spite of the Grand Duke's promised protection. The Genoese Senate had offered the large award[61] of 2,000 gold *scudi* (about £2,200) for his capture (or that of Costa or Durazzo) dead or alive; and in Tuscany there were plenty of *stiletti* for sale at that price. So, in mid-December, Theodore went to Rome, where he was befriended (and,

8

doubtless, lent some more money) by the Sisters Cassandra and Angelica Fonseca; thence, after a brief stay, he turned north—through Turin (too near Genoa), Paris* (too many unpaid debts) and Rouen—to Holland. For a few weeks he lived at The Hague with a Jew named Tellano, whose house was in a cul-de-sac by the Comédie Française; then, at the beginning of March 1737, he appears in Amsterdam.

We now begin to see the burgeoning of the ideas nascent in Theodore's fertile brain as he crossed from Corsica to Leghorn. It was not for nothing that he had issued those decrees at Sartène for the "economic development" of Corsica. Play-acting? Yes, but with a purpose already vaguely in mind. The decrees—he had Costa's next copies docketed in his travelling secretaire—gave the impression that Corsica was, or soon would be, a storehouse of wealth. It was no good, now, hoping to get anything more out of the Tunisian Jews and Greeks: Christoforo Buongiorno, who had visited Neuhoff in Florence, left no room for doubt that those hopeful "investors" were not only disappointed but very angry men. But could not Dutch *entrepreneurs* be interested? True, his last stay in Amsterdam, after Alberoni's fall and the collapse of Law's boom in Paris, had had disreputable features; but memories, Theodore fondly believed, were short. "And, after all," he said to himself, "am I not a crowned, legitimate king?"

Tellano had given Neuhoff letters to useful friends. Posing in Amsterdam as the "Baron of Savoy", he put up nominally at an inn, kept by one Ham, much frequented by ship's captains. Actually, in the interests of security, he slept each night at a different lodging—sometimes in a friend's house, sometimes in a hostelry. These precautions, which

---

* According to the *Gentleman's Magazine* of March 1737, Theodore was ordered by the French authorities to leave the Kingdom in forty-eight hours. They had apparently not forgotten earlier espionage activities.

Theodore, in talk with Tellano's friends, ascribed to "the risks of high politics", did not avail to avert disaster. Neuhoff had underrated men's memories. He soon found that, if Paris had held an inconvenient press of creditors, Amsterdam was also dangerous. In particular, the guard﹦ ians of two children, from whose dead father Theodore had borrowed years ago, were insistent on bringing him to justice. Employing a "private eye", by name von Hochum, they traced Neuhoff one night to the hostelry *Et Rode Hart*, and called[62] the police.

Arrested as a defaulting debtor, Theodore was lodged at first under guard, in private quarters where he was allowed to receive visitors. Many came to see the fallen monarch—out of pity, or curiosity. Theodore, who is recorded[63] as having received guests "with dignity, but laconically", turned for help to St Gill, the Spanish Ambassador at The Hague. He was prepared, he wrote, to cede Corsica to Don Carlos, if the King of Spain would give him a command against the Moors in Africa, and if St Gill would instruct the Spanish consul at Amsterdam to bail him out in the sum of 3,000 *pistoles*. The ambassador did not reply; and the news of Theodore's arrest brought daily fresh creditors with claims so huge that Tellano's friends, who had been seeking to raise funds for him, felt that they were confronted with an impossible task. The figure of debts in sight—some contracted in Holland, some owing to foreigners—mounted to nearly 30,000 florins. "Repayment would be as difficult as drinking the sea."

Those were bad days for Theodore. Though his arrest caused joy in Bastia, where Governor Rivarola ordered a Te Deum to be sung and tried to exploit the news by offering an amnesty and truce (which the insurgents con﹦ temptuously rejected), the Regency Council—to whom the news was carried from France by "Colonel" Colonna and

"Captain" Sinibaldi—must have been cast down by the realization that an imprisoned debtor would be unlikely to bring them quick succour in the form of arms or food. Indeed it looked for a time as if Theodore's bid to exploit his claim to a lost crown was finally defeated. With no sign to be discerned that he could ever meet any of his obligations, he was removed from his temporary quarters and cast into the regular debtors' prison in Amsterdam. There he seemed likely to rot for many months to come.

CHAPTER NINE

Operation Boon

IN the Amsterdam debtors' jail, Theodore was given—as a German nobleman, if not as a monarch whose legitimacy the States General had failed to recognize—one concession: he had pen and ink and his "papers". With these he got busy—in the drafting of a "prospectus" which would have done credit to a company promoter of modern times. Territory? The kingdom of Corsica. Resources? Limitless: an island flowing with wine, olive oil and honey; rich in salt; rapidly developing—did not the Sartène decrees prove it—a host of industries. Vendor? Why, who but the rightful elected king, beloved of his subjects? He could assign to "gentlemen adventurers" of mercantile Holland trading concessions—a monopoly, if they pleased—in this unexploited isle of plenty.

It was an ingenious proposal: little was known of Corsica in Dutch commercial circles; and, through the agency of Tellano's friends, Theodore, from behind his bars, managed to kindle the interest of a Dutch Member of Parliament, Lucas Boon, Deputy for Gelderland. Boon is described[64] as "an intriguer, versed in alchemy"; but he was evidently a man of some weight, with useful business contacts. At all events, he succeeded in forming a consortium of Dutch merchants—César Tronchin, Neufville, Daniel Dedieu and several others, mainly Jews. They agreed to put up the capital (Boon was seemingly allotted founder's shares, without cash payment, as promoter of the company) required to finance a "trading expedition" to Corsica.

The next step was to secure the release of the king. This proved unexpectedly easy. Conceivably the States General were embarrassed by their possession of this royal prisoner; indeed the Dutch Press had been officially asked[65] to "lay off" news items about Neuhoff. Possibly the Spanish Ambassador had been told by His Catholic Majesty or Don Carlos to put in a word for Theodore; and Dedieu was on friendly terms with Golowkin, the powerful Russian Envoy at The Hague. Wires evidently were pulled; and some of the more pressing creditors were paid something on account by the consortium. April 1737 saw Theodore liberated and brought before the *Cour des Echevins* to swear, in the alder-men's presence, a solemn and binding promise to meet all his debts eventually in full.

It was a strange scene. As the king, very erect, sword in belt, cane and gloves in hand, entered the chamber, the aldermen all rose to their feet, and remained standing while Theodore swore his oath. Outside a great crowd of sight-seers assembled, and the king had to be smuggled out by a side door, whence Boon's carriage took him to Dedieu's house. The Press, with Boon acting as good "public rela-tions" man, became noticeably more friendly. The *Mercure de Hollande* in its April issue was writing in glowing terms of the great potential wealth of Corsica.

The consortium then got busy. (According to Campre-don's agent in Bastia, Orticoni was advised, early in May, that "the king was on his way back".) A small ship, the *Agatha*, with a crew of twelve, was chartered at Flushing. Useful goods were purchased—two cannon, some barrels of powder, a quantity of lead, iron bars, fuses, writing-paper, cloth, and a number of muskets, pistols, trumpets and shoes. Theodore engaged as equerry a young Dutchman, by name Keverberg, whose father was a captain of Dutch dragoons. As secretary he enrolled Denis Richard, an impecunious but educated youth from Guernsey, from whose diary[66] this part of the story is drawn.

The *Agatha* was sent to Texel to load; and towards the end of June the king, with secretary and equerry, went to Den Helder, near Texel, and put up at *Het Wapen van Amsterdam*. There they were joined by Boon, who became very uneasy: there were "strange faces" about the inn's doors. The king, said Boon, had better not risk embarking openly at Texel. It would be more politic to go to Wijk-aan-Zee, with Keverberg. He should procure there a small boat and meet the *Agatha* at sea. The boat, like the *Agatha*, should fly, for the moment, the British flag.

A neat plan, but it was nearly Theodore's undoing. On June 29 Boon and Richard embarked on the *Agatha* at Texel, and sailed to pick up the king; but a violent head-wind forced them to return to Texel, whence Boon hurried on horseback to Wijk-aan-Zee to stop Theodore from put-ting off in his boat. He was too late: all that night the king and Keverberg tossed on the North Sea, looking vainly for the *Agatha*. At dawn they headed for Texel, found the *Agatha* in harbour, and got aboard. There, at 9 a.m., Boon rejoined them, and the *Agatha* made for sea at four o'clock in the afternoon.

Before going back ashore, Boon told the master, by name Barentz, that Theodore was Mijnheer Bookman, his agent in Leghorn, and that this important passenger would give him further written instructions from the charterers during the voyage to Italy. Richard observes that Barentz, who was making his first voyage as master, was a man of "limited judgment and little knowledge"; but it is doubtful if he was ignorant of Theodore's identity. In any case, on July 13, off the coast of Portugal, Richard handed Barentz a sealed letter from Boon, revealing the passenger's real name and instructing the master to put into the Tagus. Two days later, the *Agatha* anchored off the fort of Belem, just below Lisbon.

At this point Theodore's actions were curious; and his evident intentions, once again, not those of a hero. According to one kindly biographer,[67] he did not mean at this stage to return personally to Corsica: the ship was to land its cargo there, for the Regents' use, while he (Theodore) would endeavour in Lisbon and Madrid to secure further aid. Richard, however, has a different story; and though that young man, as we shall see, double-crossed his employer in the end, he may well have then felt he was justifiably "getting his own back": there is no evidence that he was a liar, and his account is first-hand and circumstantial.

What Mr Secretary Richards has to say of the call at Lisbon is that when the port health officers boarded the *Agatha*, Theodore tried to remain in his cabin—*embusqué*. As the officers insisted that they must see every passenger on the manifest, the king professed to be suffering from gout; he was aided, limping, stiffly, up the companion-ladder, dressed in an embroidered white shirt, Moroccan slippers and a white cap trimmed with beaver. Satisfied that the distinguished invalid was not infectious, the officers withdrew—not before they had got a shrewd inkling of Theodore's identity, which soon became known throughout the city. But for some days the king made no move to go ashore or approach the government: fearing either creditors or (it may be) Genoese agents, he stayed in his cabin, an attitude hardly consistent with "seeking aid" from His Catholic Majesty.

After some days, while Boon's Lisbon agents, Vernais and Cloots, were assembling more cargo, Keverberg was sent to present "Baron Kepre's" compliments to Van Sil, the Dutch resident at Lisbon. Hospitable, and doubtless moved too by curiosity, Van Sil invited the "Baron" to spend a few days at his villa by the sea—an invitation which His Majesty accepted with royal pleasure. Richard stayed on board; and Keverberg—who had so far acted as cook, apparently not to his employer's satisfaction—was bidden find a *maître-queue*. This he did in the person of Joseph Paris, a Provençal, who embarked on July 25—very fine, with sword and scarlet vest. Keverberg also picked up twenty-four deserters from the Spanish Army, who thought themselves lucky to sail from Lisbon into the unknown. By this time the loading was nearly complete—groceries, coffee, chocolate, 130 muskets and (a horrid addition to the cargo) thirty-six syringes and a large jar of nitric acid—to be squirted, it seems, without noise, against Genoese sentries. On July 27 the *Agatha* lifted her anchor, picked up Theodore from Van Sil's seaside villa (at the Estoril), and proceeded on her voyage in fine weather.

So far, so good. Theodore had a Corsican flag—the rebels' green and yellow—made of scraps of bunting from the locker; spirits were high as the *Agatha* rounded Cape St Vincent. Then came an unforeseen set-back. Barentz knew nothing of the Mediterranean, and he had no charts. Told to head for Corsica, he was completely at a loss; and the pilot, a "foxy fellow", according to Richard, professed equal ignorance. Tacking against a moderate *levanto* (east) wind, the *Agatha* presently came abreast of Oran. Galleys (were they Moors?) hove in sight. The *Agatha* hoisted the English flag. An imprudent action, as it turned out. The galleys (not Moorish, after all) raised the Spanish flag to the masthead and opened fire. Hurriedly the timorous Barentz exchanged British for Dutch colours: it was too late, too suspicious a manœuvre. The Spaniards, boarding the *Agatha*, found arms on board, suspected (naturally enough) a Dutch gun-running enterprise on the sultan's behalf, and took the ship, as legitimate prize, into Oran.

In that port, Theodore had another feigned attack of gout. To avoid "loss of face" by rising when the officers of the governor-general, the Marquis de Vallejo, came on board, the king lay on a *chaise-longue*, his foot on a stool. He may have won sympathy, even respect. But that did not prevent the impounding of the ship and the incarceration of all its company in the various Spanish castles at Oran. From that confinement—"honourable" in his own case, less so for Richard and the rest—Theodore asked for, and obtained, an interview, with Vallejo. What now? All that Vallejo would undertake to do was to send an express messenger to Madrid for instructions. He was, however, polite; and bottles of Rhine and Malaga wine were amic-ably exchanged. Meanwhile, to the fury of poor Captain Barentz, the *Agatha* was taken to Mersa and stripped of sails and rudder as a precaution against escape.

Then, on August 17, instructions came from Madrid: Theodore was to be set at liberty, his ship returned intact and ready for sea, and full compensation paid him for the expenses of his detention. The Marquis de Vallejo, full of amiable contrition, sped the party, with acclaim, on their way. Yet, sailing north with a slight, but favouring, breeze Theodore evinced (so Richard relates) symptoms of increasing "nerves": he displayed, on the most charitable view, that capacity, of which Chevrier wrote, of failing "to carry through an impetuous design". On September 2, off the Sardinian coast, a Swedish vessel, the *Great Christopher* (master, Jonas Kerhoet) was met, bound from Cagliari in Sardinia to Stockholm with salt. There were ship-to-ship

parleys. Would Captain Kerhoet take a passenger for
Holland or England? Yes, for 20 *zecchini*. The bargain was
struck; Theodore, accompanied by his equerry, Keverberg,
transhipped for the north; the *Agatha*, with Richard still
on board, bore on for Corsica.

But not, as it befell, to land her cargo. On September 6
the promontory of Bonifacio was sighted. How make a
landing? And where? Barentz was in a panic; he did not
know this dangerous coast, and the "foxy" pilot was un-
helpful. Fog rolled up. When it cleared, there were two
feluccas (almost certainly Genoese, thought Barentz) on the
horizon. Hurriedly, Barentz rolled the Corsican flag round
the jar of nitric acid and consigned this compromising
cargo to the deep blue sea. The *feluccas* drew nearer; Barentz
decided to abandon the idea of landing his cargo on an
unknown and inhospitable coast: he turned east and made
for Leghorn. And there, early on September 13, he arrived.
At once the port authorities made difficulties. Where were
the two passengers—"Bookman" and Keverberg—listed on
the manifest and now missing? "Lost at Oran" was the only
reply Barentz could make. It is improbable that the Livornese authorities believed him; but they could do nothing
about it.

The ship's company dispersed. The Spanish deserters,
poor devils, took service in the forces of the Emperor;
Barentz, urged by Corsican agents to continue his voyage
to the island, stoutly refused; Richard, stranded in Leghorn
and penniless but for such "touches" as he could make in
the counting-house of Boon's none too friendly agents, sold
his diary (for a song) to the Genoese Senate, after showing
it and telling his tale[68] to (slightly) more generous
Campredon. He then vanishes from this history.

Such was the inglorious ending of "Operation Boon".
During his leisurely stay in Van Sil's comfortable villa at

the Estoril, Neuhoff had begun to wonder whether his personal intervention in Corsica at this juncture would not be both premature and risky. He had got his backers, "*les croupiers du Roi*" in Amsterdam. Thanks to them, he was a free man again. But how petty, when all was said— and here we detect the vanity of the man—had been their investment! One paltry ship! As the *Agatha* ploughed on from Lisbon through the Straits of Gibraltar, it became clear to Theodore that it would justly take much more than that to induce him to risk his life in that turbulent island: he was not a crazy Stuart! So, let Barentz and Richard carry on to Corsica and hand the cargo over to the Regents with his blessing. The neck of a crowned king was not lightly to be risked. His part would be to return to Holland and persuade Boon's consortium that the "venture"—to ensure success—must be planned on more generous lines. This, as I have said, is a story without a hero.

CHAPTER TEN

"Will ye no' come back again?"

In that autumn of 1737, Death took a hand in the sorry affairs of King Theodore's followers. While the king was sailing on the *Great Christopher* to a destination at present undisclosed, Costa lay dying, penniless, in a Leghorn garret. Did his loyalty turn to disillusionment in the end? Did the news of Theodore's abandonment of the *Agatha* break his fortitude? There is no means of searching now the dark forest of a man's heart on which the withered leaves of two centuries have fallen. By the end of September Costa had said good-bye to his anxieties and regrets; from his last lodging in a Leghorn slum, the Grand Chancellor was carried to his grave.

His was not the only tragedy. During October, accord-ing to one chronicler,[69] an agent of Theodore's, by name Colombani, was captured on arrival in the island and tortured to death in Bastia—the partisans shooting forty Genoese prisoners outside the city walls in reprisal. But this was not all. The planners of "Operation Boon" had provided—though quite inadequately, Neuhoff had thought—for a "build-up" to support the Corsican land-ing. In June they had chartered for four months (the charter rate being agreed at 1,600 florins monthly) a vessel belonging to the Dutch firm of Splenter, van Doorn and Louxissen. Her name was the *Yong-Rombout*, and she carried eighteen guns. On this ship, with a cargo of miscellaneous munitions and stores, embarked the Florentine secretary, Francesco dell'Agata, who had landed with Theodore at Leghorn in November 1736. The ship sailed from Amsterdam on June 23, and arrived off Cap Corse about the middle of October. The master, Anton Bevers, was an experienced sailor; but neither he nor dell'Agata had had any proper briefing on the current situation in the island. The result was that, instead of reconnoitring with a view to a beach landing, the secretary put off in a small boat and rowed unsuspect-ingly into the harbour of Ile Rousse—under the impression, apparently, that the citadel was in the hands of the insur-gents. It was a costly error: dell'Agata stepped ashore and walked straight into the arms of the Genoese. The com-mandant of the garrison hanged him summarily next morning.[70]

When the boat's crew brought back to the ship the story of dell'Agata's capture, Bevers decided discreetly to sail for Naples, in the belief (not unjustified) that Don Carlos was well-disposed. Hardly was the anchor down in Naples harbour before the *Yong-Rombout* was boarded by Domenico Rivarola, the former Spanish consul at Bastia and now one of the rebels' chief agents on the mainland. Rivarola pressed Bevers to sail back to Corsica and land his cargo: even though Theodore had vanished, the muni-tions and stores embarked by *"les croupiers du Roi"* would be invaluable to Paoli and the other Regents. Bevers demurred: a beach landing would be a slow process, and he had no mind to risk capture by Genoese *feluccas*. If a substantial port were in rebel hands, it would be different.

Rivarola had to concede Bevers' point. His reaction was

to charter a *felucca* belonging to the Lipari Islands. It is typical of the commercial ingenuity which the king had taught his associates that the charter-money was borrowed from officers of the forces of Don Carlos on the strength of a promise to bring recruits from Corsica to Naples! Having put on board a small quantity of guns, powder and shot from the *Yong-Rombout*, Rivarola dispatched the *felucca* with an urgent message to the Regents, urging that every effort be made to secure Porto-Vecchio as a supply-base. On January 7, 1738, the vessel reached Monte Cristo, a little island south of Elba. There ten of the crew deserted; but the voyage continued, and Corsica was reached[71] on January 13. There is no further record of the fate of this expedition; but whether or not the arms and Rivarola's message reached Paoli, no serious effort was made then, or later, to capture a port of disembarkation for the armaments which the Dutch merchants—so Rivarola hoped—would go on adventurously dispatching. In fact, the position on the island was on the point of changing radically—and not to Theodore's advantage.

M de Campredon, the French Envoy at Genoa, had long been urging Paris (as we have seen) to recognize that Corsica was a magnet for the ambitions both of Don Carlos and Spain and also of the Maritime Powers, Britain and Holland. Though Theodore was in exile, the insurgents in the *maquis* were indomitable; and the Genoese, shut up in their garrison towns, might weary of the cost of fighting an interminable insurrection and offer the island for sale. There would be many bidders: the Spanish Envoy at Genoa, Señor Cornejo, was being "very active", said Campredon; and one must not forget the interest in Corsican affairs shown both by Grand Duke Francis of Lorraine and Charles Emmanuel, Duke of Savoy and King of Sardinia. Had not Francis, in the winter of 1736-7, hatched a plot to finance an attempt to put on Theodore's throne a disreputable creature of his, the unfrocked monk who went by the name of Humbert Beaujeu de la Salle? Was not a Colonel Boieri of the Spanish Army in the plot? And, for that matter, would not Corsica be a neat and desirable addition either to the British base of Minorca, or the Sardinian Kingdom—to the great detriment of France's naval position in the Mediterranean? How dangerous was the weakness of Genoa!

So M de Campredon—in many dispatches to Paris, and though his master, Chauvelin—had paid little attention. Amelot (who became Foreign Minister, under Fleury, in February 1737) lent a readier ear. On July 12, 1737, he signed, at Versailles, a declaration[72] to which the Emperor's Envoy, Schmerling, set his name: it would be the joint care of France and Austria to uphold the interests of Genoa in Corsica. This done, Amelot proceeded to offer the Genoese Senate military aid—on the same mercenary basis as that demanded by Austria in 1731. The offer was accepted—with the usual Genoese grumblings at the price—and on November 10, 1737, a convention was signed at Foun-tainebleau by Amelot and Sorba, the Genoese Envoy to Louis XV. France would dispatch a contingent of 3,000 men, with a reinforcement of 5,000 more, if needed. The cost to Genoa would be proportionate to the numbers sent, but would not exceed two million French *livres*.

There is reason to suppose that Amelot, at this stage, was playing a double game. He did not want Corsica to fall into Spanish (or any other power's) hands through Genoese collapse; but he did not see any advantage in turning the people of Corsica into irreconcilable enemies of France, who might, one day, want to absorb the island as painlessly as possible. Cardinal Fleury had received recently a long letter[73] from a priest, Gregorio Salvini, who had become one of the rebels' chief agents in Leghorn. With the "justice" of the Corsicans' cause which Salvini had pleaded (making no reference, incidentally, to Theo-dore) Fleury was probably not much concerned. But Amelot enjoyed careful fishing in troubled waters. M Pignon, the French consul at Tunis, was transferred to Leghorn with instructions to watch matters, make all useful contacts and report fully and regularly. At the same time, the Comte de Boissieux, appointed to command the French expedition, was given a directive to act "diplomatically" and see if he could not quench the rebellion by a judicious blend of firmness and tactful negotiations.

Ships and troops assembled at Antibes; and on February 1, 1738, the flotilla sailed, with the frigate *La Flore* (thirty guns), carrying the flag of the Comte de Pardaillon, at the head of the line. On board was a M Jaussin, naval apothecary-doctor, whose recollections[74] combine with M Pignon's and M de Campredon's reports to furnish us with a circumstantial account of some of the events of that year. The weather was windless, the voyage slow; but, on February 6, Bastia was reached and disembarkation begun at 4 p.m. From the outset, Franco-Genoese relations were bad. Boissieux disliked Mari, the new Genoese Governor at Bastia; he complained bitterly to Campredon that his men were lodged like dogs. Mari, in turn, reported acidly to the Republic that his agents were continually intercepting "treasonable" correspondence between the French general and the insurgents.

There is evidence[75] that negotiations between Boissieux and Giafferi were so amicable that the Corsican at one point offered to open a market near Bastia for the benefit of the French troops. (There would, if we are to believe one story,[76] have been a good prospect of a truce if the Corsicans had not insisted on the return of "our King"—a demand

9

which Fleury refused.) Negotiations with Giafferi would
in fact fit in with Boissieux's directive; and it seems likely
that Pignon was acting, in Leghorn, along similar lines.
At any rate, about this time, Salvini was writing[77] to
Canon Orticoni in Corsica and urging that the Regents
should open *pourparlers* with the French.

> "*Je ne vous dirai rien de Theodore, parce que vous savez ma
> façon de penser sur son sujet, si ce n'est que vous et moi n'avons pas
> été sa dupe.*"

The canon, it seems, felt equally free from the error of
having been "taken in" by Theodore; for he replied at once
that he agreed with Salvini's advice—quite apart from the
deep respect and affection he had (heaven knows why!) for
Louis XV. It was idle, said Orticoni, any longer to expect
aid from Don Carlos or Madrid; and there was nothing to
hope for from King Theodore, "*en lequel je n'ai jamais eu
confiance*". Meanwhile, however, the single-hearted partisans
went on fighting ineffectively and bitterly. It is recorded[78]
that in one skirmish, near Bastia, a Genoese lieutenant,
Corsican by birth and suspected of an anti-Theodore
attitude, was captured by the rebels, had his tongue torn
out and finished life in a slow bonfire of damp wood.

Where was Neuhoff all these months, while fate was
condemning his "subjects" to the doubly heavy task of
contending not merely with Genoa but with a strong
French expeditionary force? He did not publicize his
movements; indeed he covered his tracks with every care,
and such letters from him in this period as survive bear
no address. In December 1737, according to Pignon,[79]
Theodore's companion on the *Great Christopher*, young
Keverberg, was found to be lodging in Lisbon. Was
Neuhoff with him? None of his friends could say. Sister
Angelica Fonseca was writing frequently in the autumn of

1737 to Captain Bigani of Leghorn, whose son had been one of the Italians who sailed in Captain Dick's ship for Tunis in 1736. What news of the poor baron? Her prayers were for his safety and victorious return. Captain Bigani unhappily could not enlighten her as to Theodore's where-abouts.

Nor did the king give any inkling of his address in letters which (Janssin records) he wrote in November 1737, to his *chère amie*, Mlle Champigny, now lodging in the Rue de la Poterie, Paris. Sending her a lengthy (and quite fictitious) list of members of the famous Order of Libera-tion which he had created a year before at Sartène, he begged for urgent news of French intentions. Was it true, as rumoured, that an expedition would shortly be sent to aid the Genoese oppressing his kingdom? The reply should kindly be sent through Baron von Drost, Grand Com-mander of the Teutonic Order (*Deutsche Ritter*) at Cologne.

In this "cover address" Mlle Champigny, had she but known it, was given a clue to Theodore's real whereabouts. Dropping Keverberg at Lisbon, her first port of call, the *Great Christopher* eventually reached Hamburg, where the king inconspicuously disembarked. Prudently, he decided not to go straight to Amsterdam: it would be wiser, first, to discover, by correspondence, how the land lay there. For the moment, his indulgent cousin's lodging in Cologne—the *Deutsche Ritter* were a law unto themselves and no policeman would dare venture his nose in those doors—promised comfort and security. There Theodore went and, having told a tale of wrongs and hardships bravely borne, obtained—for is not blood thicker than water?—the Grand Commander's forgiveness and hospitality. Once more the travelling *secretaire* was opened: ink flowed from that ingenious pen.

Thus *embusqué*, Neuhoff's very existence—and they

hardly dared hope the rogue was dead—continued to be a
worry both to the Genoese and their new allies, the French.
While Captain Bevers on the *Yong-Rombout* waited and
waited in Naples for news that Porto-Vecchio had been
"made good" for his ship to discharge, the Marquis de
Puisieux, French Ambassador to the Court of Don Carlos,
was lecturing Valemberg, the Dutch consul, with *hauteur*
and severity. The States General really must not take sides
in a rebellion by the subjects of Genoa, a republic with
which Holland was on terms of amity. (Puisieux clearly
believed, as others did later, with better grounds, that the
Dutch Government was party to the speculative adventures
of Messrs Boon and Dedieu.) Bevers himself was threatened
by French and Genoese agents with short shrift if he ventured to sail for Corsica and was caught. At length, in
March 1738, the poor captain's worries were ended: he got
instructions from Amsterdam to sail for Leghorn and
unload both his cargo and the ship's guns. This he did, and
fades out of this story.

Meanwhile, Neuhoff's pen had been busy, to good effect.
First, in October 1737, he sent an emissary to Lucas Boon
in Amsterdam with a letter of greetings and a message for
the consortium. The "export trade" of Corsica (which he
had entrusted, for the moment, to his "faithful Regents")
was taking a little time to develop: the merchants must really
exercise reasonable patience. Moreover, he added, it was
useless to stint a great venture of this sort. Barentz, Richard,
and that imprudent idiot from Florence had made a mess
of things; but, after all, bricks could not be made without
straw: the resources at their disposal had been quite inade-
quate. As it was, with the damned French now reinforcing
the Genoese, an even bigger expedition would be needed.
But, wrote Theodore, "I have in my mind an excellent
plan, and it has the positive backing of Don Carlos."

Could Boon assure him that, if he came to Amsterdam to unfold the details, there would be no more "unpleasantness" over those unpaid debts?

Boon, who was no fool, by now suspected that he was dealing with a crook rather than a king; but he did not communicate his suspicions to the rest of the consortium. After all, he had not risked any of his own money in the *Agatha*; and, as "public relations man", with his influence in Parliament, he might yet get a few pickings at his associates' expense. To Neuhoff he wrote back that he was "interested". Let Theodore come to Amsterdam with a stout lacquey or two borrowed from his cousin's household: the matter of the creditors and the pledges of repayment made to the *Echevins* would be "taken care of".

Back in Amsterdam, Theodore lost no time in unfolding his scheme to Boon, Tronchin, Dedieu and the rest. Why, he suggested, should not his kingdom—his by legitimate right of election—be converted into a "private colony" for right-minded Dutch merchants in whose hearts the conception of liberty was cherished? Colonists had fructified America: why not Corsica? Blood from northern strains —here Theodore grew lyrical—would invigorate the race in that lush, exotic *dolce far niente* island, with all its great, only half-developed resources. The States General would surely help in providing an armada.

Regarded coolly, from the distance of two centuries, the scheme hatched by Neuhoff seems fantastic—too extravagant in its false pretences regarding the resources of his barren, mountainous island to have made any impression on a group of Dutch merchants. But this, I repeat, was the age of the South Sea Bubble, of appetites itching for new worlds, of brains afire with crackpot schemes. Boon, thinking of his commission on purchases, his rake-off from squaring Government officials and the newspapers, was

impressively favourable. The rest were greedy. Incredible
though it now seems, the consortium adopted the "prospectus"; they were almost eager to throw good money after bad.

The news spread. In February 1738 Pignon was
writing[80] to Amelot that an agent of the king had recently
arrived in Corsica with some arms and the news that
Theodore would soon be "back again". Meanwhile, by a
strange coincidence with which we must connect guilders
discreetly distributed by Lucas Boon, the Dutch newspapers
began to carry stories extolling Corsica and its "grain, wine
and oil, whose abundance makes their prices ridiculously
low". The *"croupiers du Roi"*, joined now by a new associate,
Mijnheer Vandermil, had begun to get busy in the game of
"making a market" for a new enterprise.

The highlands of Scotland were not more stirred, a few
years later, by rumours of the Young Pretender's movements
than the French and Genoese were in Corsica, that spring,
by reports of Theodore's impending arrival. The Regents,
sharing (one surmises) Canon Orticoni's scepticism,
showed no overt sign of enthusiasm; but M Pignon—moved
by Amelot, in March, to Bastia, so as to be more "on the
spot"—was greatly excited. Complaining to Amelot that
Boissieux had become "pro-Corsican" (ah, these soldiers!
Shades of T. E. Lawrence and Wingate!), he reported,[81]
first, the arrival at Aleria of "Prosper de Matris" a Dutch
lord, obviously(!) Theodore. Then, when this *canard*
proved false, he had "red-hot" news of the arrival, in late
April, of "Matthieu Drost", Theodore's "nephew".

This character, whose real name is unknown, was not a
member of the noble Drost family of Westphalia, but a
shady adventurer, one of a motley gang of crooks, headed
by the "Chevalier St Martin" (*alias* Bigou), Duffour and
Gio Ludovici, who had clutched Theodore's coat-tails in
Leghorn, a year earlier. Landing in Corsica[82] on April 30,

with letters from Theodore for the chieftains, he had a cold reception at a meeting at Casinca; and, after appealing vainly to Boissieux for a safe-conduct, managed by the skin of his teeth to make his way to the coast, where a fishing-boat took him to Leghorn. There, according to Mr Consul Goldsworthy,[83] he was arrested, but had nothing of importance to impart, and was soon released.

Amelot quickly grew tired of M Pignon's excitable reports from Bastia; and still less did he care for his criticism of Boissieux. He recalled his agent in a singularly stiff missive:[84] his services had become "*inutiles*". The Foreign Minister was content with the more objective and cynical reports of M de Campredon, who had just regaled his master with a story of the Genoese capture, in the hills near Savona, of a poor lunatic whom they took for the King of Corsica! Rumours, reports—and growing suspicion of the motives of the Dutch Government: so passed the spring of 1738 in the Genoese sphere. The king would "come back again". Had it been known to M de Campredon what was really afoot in Amsterdam, he might have shared poor M Pignon's excitement.

CHAPTER ELEVEN

The Armada of 1738

THEODORE had suggested to his "sleeping partners" in Amsterdam that, as part of the "colonizing" venture, they should recruit "artisans" for service in Corsica: the new industries needed skilled hands! The *croupiers* saw no point in adhering strictly to technical definitions of skill; they but endorsed the king's grand conception. If the Pilgrim Fathers, in 1620, had taken ship for the unknown West, why should not emigrants from a none-too-prosperous Europe in 1738 sail, as Dutch-sponsored pioneers, to a Mediterranean island so rich[85] in "wine, grain and olive oil"? And if, at first, the "artisans" had to do a little soldiering, would not their reward—in heaven, if not on earth—be all the greater?

To make the answer to this question convincingly affirmative, Theodore and Lucas Boon, engaged, in January 1738, a small corps of recruiting agents. There was Jonias von Bessel, a Prussian; Captain Ludwik, also from Prussia, recently released from a Dutch jail; one Kraam, background unknown; and a woman, name unrecorded. They worked hard to earn their pay. Ludwik enrolled Johann-Gottfried Water, aged thirty-eight, a Saxon, married, and with a son aged eleven. He had served in the

Emperor's Army, and was engaged, with a promise of a "company command" in Corsica, at a salary of 50 florins a month. Kraam, a less effectively spell-binding recruiter, had to fall back on his own family: his trove was a young relative, Johann-Gottlieb Reusse, a student of engineering at Leyden. He took service under Theodore as "Engineer-Officer" at 25 florins a month—a salary promised also to Tobais-Fredericus Boller of Württemberg, who came to Amsterdam in quest of adventure and was lured by Theodore's "literature" puffing the Corsican enterprise. The rest came cheaper. Kaspar Wirt of Cologne, who had arrived in Amsterdam a day too late to catch his ship for the Indies, accepted engagement for "general duties" at 14 florins a month, rather than be stranded in Holland. (The anonymous woman agent picked him up.) Others, many others—the flotsam of Amsterdam—followed suit, for even less remunerative engagements. Quite a little company of "colonist-adventurers" was assembled by April.

Meanwhile, Boon had been active in chartering a fleet. This time it was a substantial armada. First there was the *Agatha*, of whose previous exploits we have read, now carrying sixteen guns (master, Adolphus Peresen). Then came a similar ship, the *Marie-Jacob* (twelve guns; master, Cornelius Roos). Bulkier, and more heavily armed, was the *African*, with forty guns, whose master, Pieter Keelman, had a one-fourth share in the whole adventure. Finally, as flag ship to the convoy, without cargo, Boon had somehow managed to charter[86] the *Brederode* (sixty guns; master, Alexander Frentzel), a superannuated Dutch naval ship-of-the-line. It is difficult to avoid the suspicion that officials of the States General, "squared" by Boon, must have quietly blessed the expedition.

The cargo loaded on this fleet was varied, bellicose and considerable. According to a bill of lading circulated later in Corsica (it was drafted by Theodore and is therefore suspect) and found by Jaussin, the naval apothecary,[87] the *African, Marie-Jacob* and *Agatha* carried, between them, 24 cannon, 3 culverins, 6,000 muskets, 4,000 pistols and a great quantity of powder, shot, bandoliers and trumpets—to say nothing of more syringes to implement Theodore's notions (novel in 1738) of chemical warfare waged with nitric acid. The ships also loaded considerable quantities of commercially saleable grain, clothing and shoes, together with a large number of empty casks for the homeward transport of olive oil. Altogether, it seems, the Amsterdam merchants staked about £40,000 on this venture—no mean sum in those days.

On May 20 the *Marie-Jacob*, escorted by the *Brederode*, put to sea, followed, two days later, by the *Agatha*. The *African*, her loading not complete, was to sail later and join the others at Cagliari in Sardinia. On the *Brederode* was Theodore, accompanied by his cousin, so-called "Colonel", Friederich von Neuhoff, and his retinue. The ship's company included a sailor, François Vastel, to whose subsequent testimony, supported by that of a German sailor, by name Riesenberg, on the *African*, and the depositions[88] of others in the enterprise, our knowledge of this strange Odyssey is largely due.

The *Brederode* and the two transports called at Malaga and Alicante for water. At the latter port, according to Vastel, Theodore had undertaken to pay the captain and crew an advance of wages. Pay-day came, but no money. Only reluctantly was Captain Frentzel persuaded to continue his voyage. At sea, Vastel (so he tells us) had been in trouble with the mate: being a Catholic, he had refused to attend the Protestant services on board. Theodore, he says, took his part against the mate, and gave him a present of two *ducats*: if he remained steadfast and loyal, he should

have a "command" in Corsica (Theodore was never nig-
gardly in promises, and his generosity was usually calculated
—even to the volume of two *ducats*.)

After Alicante, according to Vastel's account, the fleet—
Brederode, Agatha and *Marie-Jacob*—carried out a curious
manœuvre. Instead of sailing direct for Corsica, the ships
headed south and called at Algiers. The two transports
cruised outside (*au large*) and the *Brederode* alone entered the
port, where she stayed for a fortnight. The Dutch consul
was a frequent visitor on board—a circumstance which lent
further colour to French suspicions that this armada (including an ex-navy battleship) could hardly have left Holland
without some official connivance. Theodore and the consul
had long talks out of Keelman's hearing. After that, sail was
made again for the north. On August 14 the fleet anchored
in the harbour of Cagliari; and, two days later, the *African*
arrived. Cagliari was agog. Mongiardino, the Genoese
consul, sent an urgent message of warning[89] to Governor
Mari at Bastia; and similar letters were dispatched to
General Boissieux by the French consul and by the Marquis
de Rivarola, Charles-Emmanuel's viceroy in Sardinia. The
arrival of this heavily armed flotilla meant clearly that the
Corsican fat would soon be in the fire.

So it might have been. Even if Theodore's "bill of lading"
exaggerated the cargoes, the rebels were on the way to
receiving a reinforcement of supplies which could have
seriously worried Boissieux and the Genoese. But now
comes—as always in the Summer King's career—an anti-
climax of deception and chicanery. On August 20 the
Agatha and *Marie-Jacob* sailed north from Cagliari, followed
a few hours later (when darkness had fallen) by the *African*
and the flagship *Brederode*. Theodore had meanwhile transhipped from the *Brederode* to the *African*. Why? According
to Vastel, there was "deadly sickness" on the *Brederode*,

whose captain, having escorted his convoy to the Straits of
Bonifacio, stood on for Port Mahon in Minorca, where
medical aid might be had. There Vastel deserted from the
Brederode, and eventually got passage on a French *tartane*
(master, Alexandre Boyer) trading out of Martigues; on
this craft he reached Alicante, where he told his tale to the
French consul.

Meanwhile, on the *African*, with the coast of Corsica in
sight and the familiar beaches round Aleria distant only by
a few hours' sailing, Theodore issued astonishing orders:
let Captain Keelman port his helm and make for Naples.
Did the king have a fit of "nerves", shrink—once again—
physically from the dangers of a landing in a rude kingdom
which he had quitted nearly two years ago? I fear the true
explanation is that he had never really intended to go to
Corsica, but meant always to sell most of his backers'
cargo in the easier market of Naples. For the moment,
however, this attempt by Theodore once more to double-
cross his backers was defeated by Keelman. That stiff Dutch
captain, with £10,000 at stake in the trading venture,
wanted his olive oil. Bidding Theodore hold his tongue, he
stood on, past Bonifacio, up the east coast of the island.

On that day, the ill-omened thirteenth of September, an
odd incident befell—or so, at least, Riesenberg records in
his diary. A multi-coloured bird circled the *African* and
dropped, as if lifeless, on the deck at Theodore's feet. The
king picked it up; whereupon the bird recovered and flew
off towards the Corsican mountains—a bad augury, so the
ship's company thought, though their process of reasoning
is not clear.

Next day, the three transports anchored off the little port
of Sorraco, near Porto-Vecchio. From there, Theodore—
pinned by the obdurate Keelman to his proclaimed purpose—wrote to the Marquis Xaviero di Matra, his earliest

adherent. "In spite of treachery and persecutions," the letter[90] ran, "I have returned, safe and sound." Would Xaviero please send men, armed or unarmed, together with horses for the king and his retinue, and 200 baggage mules? Arms and ammunition would be distributed *gratis*, but the fleet's cargo of cloth, shoes, iron and copper would be available only on a barter basis—against local products, notably olive oil. Xaviero, who (as previously related) had deserted his monarch in the summer of 1736, must have wondered whether he was being invited to join in a liberation crusade or a commercial auction mart. Another message[91] was dispatched by the king that day to Napoleoni Talese, the *curé* of Porto-Vecchio. Complaining that the parishioners of the *curé* had turned "collaborators", Theodore promised pardon for their offences if they sent hostages for their good behaviour.

No reply came from Xaviero. A few partisans gathered on the beach, shouted *"Vive le Roi"*, and came off in small boats for a gift of ammunition; but for three days, obviously uncertain of his reception, Theodore stayed on board the *African*, while Keelman (according to Riesenberg) became more and more angry at the delays. Eventually, on September 18, at three o'clock in the afternoon, the royal party disembarked. There were cheers from a little crowd of insurgents on shore, who were treated at once to a curious spectacle.

During the voyage a recruited Westphalian colonist, a café waiter by the name of Wickmannshausen, now ranking as captain, had apparently tried to kill the king.[92] Kept in irons on board, he was now brought ashore, tied to a tree, and riddled with bullets. Once again, as in the affair of Luccioni, Theodore had a gust of anger, a ruthlessness pardonable only in a man of integrity. The episode perhaps shocked Mijnheer Boon, because the *Mercure de*

Hollande's subsequent (obviously "inspired") comment was that the king had "shewn clemency": condemned to be burned alive, it reported, Wickmannshausen "had only been impaled!" But a few cheers and a staged execution were hardly a glorious return for an exiled monarch; that night was spent by Theodore back on board the *African*, awaiting developments.

Next day, September 19, "General" Luc Ornano and two priests, Dr Theodorini and another, arrived at Sorraco; and the numbers of insurgents on shore had swollen to at least 2,000. Landing of small arms and ammunition began, but there was no sign—nor could one have been expected—of olive oil for shipment, as counter-part for Dutch supplies, on that lonely coast. Keelman got seriously worried: his stake in the enterprise was obviously in jeopardy. On September 22 he halted the disembarka-tion of cargo, and next day he put out to sea, followed by the *Marie-Jacob* and *Agatha*.

Now comes an episode which does singularly little credit to Theodore. During the stay at Sorraco, a sailing smack (Jaussin describes it as a "pink") had been hired for 85 *zecchini* a month, payable in advance. The name of the smack was the *Jesus-Marie-Joseph*; that of her skipper, Roch Malato. Before leaving Sorraco, Theodore had ordered his cousin Friedrich to tranship from the *African* to the *Jesus-Marie-Joseph*, in company with Water and his wife and child, Reusse, Wirt, Tobias Boller, a "Captain" Groeben, the German sailor Riesenberg, and a number of other colonists. Some of these sailed in one of a small flotilla of four Sicilian *feluccas* which, by chance or pre-arrangement, had turned up at Sorraco.

By dawn on September 24 the armada—three transports and the five small sailing craft—were off Bonifacio. Orders came from the *African* that the *Jesus-Marie-Joseph* and three

of the Sicilian *feluccas* were to reconnoitre the west coast
in the direction of Ajaccio against which, according to
various accounts,[93] Luc Ornano had been instructed by
Theodore to launch a land attack. (Probably the idea was
to ascertain if a landing at Propriano was feasible; or so at
least Friedrich may have supposed.) The king, the orders
ran, would join the advance party next day in the fourth
Sicilian *felucca*, and the big ships would follow.

That was the last that cousin Friedrich and his companions saw of the king. On September 25, while they lay
at anchor somewhere between Propriano and Ajaccio, the
expected *felucca* arrived—with a letter from Theodore: the
party was to land and join Luc Ornano. Friedrich was
furious, according to Riesenberg; and well he might be:
there was little food on the *Jesus-Marie-Joseph*, and he had no
maps. After a day and a night of angry indecision, several
small ships, taken to be Genoese, hove in sight. The die
was cast for a landing: the whole party—"18 officers,
3 trumpets, 3 tailors and 1 mason" is Riesenberg's contemptuous description—went ashore and hid in the *maquis*
for the night, while the *Jesus-Marie-Joseph* cruised in the
offing.

Next day there was no sign of the Genoese—nor of
the Sicilians: they had made off in the night. Signals were
made to the *Jesus-Marie-Joseph*, and the party re-embarked.
The weather became bad; there was little to eat: for six days
a miserable and increasingly hungry company of adventurers
cruised aimlessly northwards. On October 3 they were in
the Gulf of Sagone, when enemy ships, unmistakably
French, this time, bore down on them; Roch Malato
hurriedly ran his craft on a sandy beach; Colonel Neuhoff
led his party up the steep tracks to Vico.

There, for a couple of days, they found shelter in a Franciscan monastery, until the prior, alarmed at the risk of

discovery by Genoese spies, insisted that his dangerous guests must leave. A desperate effort was then made to cross the mountains and reach Orezza, where Ornano was believed now to be. There were stragglers, the party broke up. Friedrich von Neuhoff somehow reached the east coast and thence got a passage to Leghorn. Hopelessly lost in the mountains, and living for days on a diet of raw chestnuts, Riesenberg, in company with the Waters, Boller and another, managed to retrace the way back to Vico.

From there a message was sent to the French consul at Ajaccio: they would surrender if their lives were spared. This was promised by the consul, and confirmed by Captain de Sabran, now commanding the *La Flore* frigate in Ajaccio harbour. Joined by Reusse, Wirt and some others, the colonists made their way on October 14 to Ajaccio, were taken by Sabran to Bastia, and there kindly treated by the French. After interrogation by M. La Ville-heurnois, the *commissaire de guerre*, the party was shipped to Toulon and released—with a little money to help their homeward journey.

Theodore, it is painfully clear, never meant to effect a landing in support of his reconnoitring party. Persuading Keelman that Don Carlos would embark a regiment if they reached the port of Naples, he deliberately made cast-aways of his cousin and the wretched colonists because he had no money for their pay, had no real use for their services, and wished (as his attempted change of plan on August 21 strongly suggests) to be free to dispose of some of his cargo—no matter how fraudulently—in a better market than Corsica. The flight from Bonifacio was hurried. Barely was the *Jesus-Marie-Joseph* out of sight on September 24 than the *African* and her consorts were set on an easterly course.[94] A fortnight later the *African* dropped her anchor off Procida; the Dutch consul, Valembergh, who had been "tipped off"—one now realizes—at Neuhoff's instance, by his colleague at Algiers, came off in a boat and had a lengthy conference with Theodore. After this, Captain Keelman moved his ship into Naples harbour, where the *Agatha* and *Marie-Jacob* had already tied up.

For some days nothing happened—nothing, at least, beyond increasingly angry words between the king and Keelman, who demanded to know where Don Carlos's regiment was, and who would pay for the cargoes. Then, on October 21, the Corsican agent, Domenico Rivarola, came on board and conducted Theodore ashore, where he remained—to Keelman's increasing disquiet. Three days later, Valembergh reappeared and invited Keelman to confer with the king at his lodging in the city. No sooner was he off his ship than the luckless captain was arrested by the Neapolitan police and clapped in jail, where Rivarola and Valembergh endeavoured by threats to persuade him to return to Corsica and put on the beach the guns and ammunition in the cargoes—without payment. The general stores were to be landed at Naples—"for disposal".

In vain did Keelman try to get messages, appealing for justice, to Montalegro, the Minister of Don Carlos. Valembergh was implacable; and when Peresen and Roos, the masters of the other two transports, declined to hand *their* cargoes over to Theodore, "for disposal", they too were arrested at the consul's instance. All three captains might well have rotted in jail for ever but for French intervention. The strange doings of the Dutch consul, whose useful services had been "bought" by Theodore, quickly got to the ears of the attentive M de Campredon, who reported[95] to his Minister in Paris. Amelot was indignant, and made prompt and stiffly worded *démarches*, both to the States General and to Montalegro. On December 5 the captains were released; and Keelman sailed for Smyrna.

Meanwhile Theodore, through the good offices of his loyal friend, Sister Angelica Fonseca, had found shelter for a time in a convent in Naples. Later he moved to the Dutch consul's house, where "Mathieu Drost", that discreditable adventurer, turned up. Then, fearing that Genoese agents in Naples might assassinate him, he evolved an ingenious device: he arranged with Montalegro (to whom he gave the impression that the correspondence in his travelling secretaire seriously compromised Don Carlos) that he should be "taken into custody". Arrested during the night of December 2–3, by Perelli (one of Don Carlos's counsellors) and forty grenadiers, he was conducted, very haughty and wearing his best suit, under guard to the citadel of Gaeta and honourably lodged in security—with all his compromising papers. There, for the moment, we leave him.

CHAPTER TWELVE

Entry of Perfidious Albion

F O U R years were to elapse before the King of Corsica—*"le roi du carrousel"*, as d'Angelo had once called him—reappeared, in a bizarre farewell performance, once more before the footlights of the European stage.* By that time great events—war between England and Spain; the death of Charles VI and the wars of the Austrian Succession; growing enmity between England and France—had occurred to shape the pattern of Theodore's manœuvres. In the interregnum, 1739–42, his doings are obscure and his contacts difficult to establish. But before we come to those dark years in the adventurer's career, and their astonishing sequel under the White Ensign, there falls to be recorded an episode in Corsica whose protagonist—exceptional in this tale of knavery and betrayals—cut an heroic figure.

In the autumn of 1738, General the Count de Boissieux had continued his efforts at peace-making. During November he made a formal offer[96] of terms to the insurgents. There would be a general amnesty, surrender of all

---

* He was not wholly forgotten in Holland. A writer whose pen name was Joli Coeur d'Argent Court, published two satiric histories, *De Gekroonde Moff* (The Crowned German) and *De Dwalende Moff* (The Travelling German): Utrecht, 1739 and 1740. See illustration facing p. 84.

arms, cancellation of all tax arrears, and no more sending of delinquents to "the Gallies" except after due trial at Genoa. (The despotic power of the governors at Bastia to "bind and let loose" had been one of the rebels' bitterest grievances.) In addition, Boissieux went on, Corsica should have a Supreme Tribunal of her own, composed of three impartial "foreign" (presumably French) judges, "neither Corsicans nor Genoese". Finally, new schools should be established in the island.

Would the Genoese have honoured such an agreement? In view of their past record, scepticism is legitimate. But the matter was not put to the test. Though Canon Orticoni was ready to accept these conditions, the other chiefs were hesitant; and the negotiations were broken off by Boissieux, shortly before Christmas, after a French company had walked into an ambush at Borgo, near Bastia, and had been badly cut up. Early in January, currency was given[97] to a document allegedly signed at "Tavignia" (presumably Tavagna) by Paoli and Giafferi. It ran, in its contemporary English version:

> We did some years ago chuse Lord Theodore, Baron of Neuhoff, King of the Island of Corsica. . . . To him we now submit and do intend for ever hereafter to submit to his person, whom God preserve, as also to his Descendants. . . . We never had it in our View or Thoughts to retract the inviolable Election of his said Majesty.

Were these really the words of Paoli and Giafferi? The declaration may, of course, have been issued by the chiefs as a new gesture of defiance to the Genoese and their French mercenaries; but the wording is suspiciously flattering to Theodore. One has a strong suspicion that the document was penned by his hand and circulated as propaganda.

In any event, it had no effect on the French. Boissieux,

ill and worried by his lack of success, died on February 2
at Bastia. His successor, the Marquis de Maillebois, landed
at Calvi on March 21, with a sterner directive[98] from Paris:
there must be no more appeasement of the rebels, and the
coast must be rigorously patrolled (M de Campredon had
told Amelot of his suspicions that the Genoese were not
above giving the insurgents clandestine help, in the way of
arms and food, against the French). The new general was
also enjoined to exact reprisals both for the ambush at
Borgo and for the losses suffered by a mixed French and
Genoese force on March 12 at Monte Maggiore, near
Calenzana.

The coastal patrol could not have been very effective; for,
on April 19, a *felucca* came inshore near Aleria, and landed
Baron Johann-Friedrich von Neuhoff, Freiherr von
Rauschenburg. The baron is described in contemporary
accounts as Theodore's "nephew", but in the statement
(see p. 190) issued in Cologne in 1740, the king speaks of
him with approbation as his cousin, "the son of my father's
brother", holding in Corsica the rank of "Lt-General".
To avoid confusion with the "Colonel" Friedrich von
Neuhoff of the previous chapter, it will be best to call him
Rauschenburg. He was young, attractive, fond of sport;
and he brought with him letters[99] from Theodore (most of
which fell into French hands) addressed to various
Corsican chiefs "beyond the mountains".

In one letter the king instructed Zenobio Paretti, commanding the insurgents at Zicavo, to seize Porto-Vecchio;
in another, addressed to "Count" Ornano, Theodore urged
the value of maintaining a tight investment of Ajaccio.
Finally, writing to his "First Chaplain", Gio Maria
Balizone Teodorini, the exiled monarch complained
bitterly of "disloyal" feuds and factions. Arrighi and Paoli
had made cause against him with the treacherous Salvini

and Canon Orticoni. (Maillebois comments[100] here that this faction now wanted to sell Corsica outright to Don Carlos.) Teodorini was to tell the king's subjects that he insisted on "obedience and fidelity". Given that, "I shall not abate my efforts for their deliverance". As soon as Porto-Vecchio was secured, a fleet would sail from Naples with munitions. Promises were always cheap with Theodore.

Had this letter reached his hands, instead of those of General Maillebois, Teodorini might well have been sceptical about that "fleet". The islanders had presumably been informed by Domenico Rivarola of the discreditable doings at Naples. Howbeit, some recipients of Theodore's letters turned up at Aleria and conducted Rauschenburg hospitably to a village in the foot-hills between Cervione and Bastia. There a boar hunt was organized for his entertainment. Things went merrily—for all, that is, save the boars—until the beaters flushed a French deserter in the *maquis*. He had an alarming (and true) tale to tell of heavy French reinforcements landing at Calvi, and a plan by Maillebois to burn out the rebels in their mountains. The hunt disintegrated; and on his return to his lodging, Rauschenburg found that his bedroom had been pillaged: 900 *zecchini* and all his clothes had gone.

The writer of a report[101] on this incident from Bastia to Marshal Belleisle in Paris expressed the view that the chiefs had "organized" the disappearance of the German's effects in order to keep him as a powerless hostage in their hands, a surety for the king's return. This seems too Machiavellian to be plausible, and it is doubtful whether the Corsicans were so anxious to have their monarch back; but at all events Rauschenburg was not otherwise ill-treated. A few days later, on May 6, he was allowed to attend a meeting of the chiefs at Venzolasca, Theodore's old headquarters; and, as a result of a spirited "No surrender" speech which he delivered, a proposal to open negotiations with Maille-bois was defeated. From Venzolasca, Rauschenburg went to the Balagne and did his best, with the local Resistance, to oppose the offensive opened by Maillebois.

French numbers and fire-power won; there was an armistice, coupled with an amnesty; and in July, Giafferi, Paoli and several other chiefs left[102] the island for Leghorn. Driven deeper and deeper into the mountains, Rauschen-burg, with a handful of "hard-core" rebels from the Balagne and Corte, tried vainly to make a stand near Zicavo, but finally had to take refuge in the forest-clad slopes of Monte Coscione, just north of the Incudine, where poor Costa had suffered so abominably on his last march with Theodore in November 1736.

There, for a year, Rauschenburg managed to maintain himself, living—none too scrupulously, one fancies—the life of a solitary bandit. Maillebois offered a reward of 3,000 *livres*—a princely sum to the Corsicans—for his capture. No Corsican tried to earn it: Prince Charlie, in a like matter, was not better served in Scotland. Finally, in September 1740, a priest, acting as intermediary for Maillebois, told Rauschenburg that if he went to the coast and picked up a passage for Italy, the French would turn a blind eye on his movements. A month later, the Freiherr landed at Leghorn—in rags. He was aided and entertained hospitably by officers of the Austrian forces there. Not beyond his deserts: his enterprise may have been folly and himself a dupe, but he had the saving virtue of courage.

Meanwhile, on the larger stage of European affairs, friction between Spain and England over trade with the West Indies was creating a situation beyond Premier Walpole's control. The loss of Jenkins's famous ear became, for the English, an issue of national prestige—just as Spanish pride was affronted by the continual "provocative" cruising of Admiral Haddock's squadron in the Mediterranean. Despite the Anglo-Spanish Convention of January 1739, in which an indemnity for Jenkins was balanced by compensation for Admiral Byng's aggression, years ago, at Cape Passaro, war-fever grew in London. Newcastle, the Secretary of State, suspected Spain (quite unjustly) of having concluded an alliance against England. In July, George II's Envoy, Keene, was recalled from Madrid; on October 19, to the ringing of the church bells which Walpole found so inapposite, war against Spain was declared—with repercussions later, as we shall see, on the fortunes of King Theodore.

The war naturally brought an increase of British naval activity in the Mediterranean. France was neutral; but General Maillebois, in Bastia, was not happy. He did not care for the activities of Mr Goldsworthy, the British consul at Leghorn, nor for the attitude of General Wachtendonck, commanding the Austrian troops in Tuscany. The Grand Duke Francis, as M de Campredon had warned Amelot, had long had his eye on Corsica; and the British might well want the island to supplement Minorca as a naval base. Most "suspiciously", he wrote, Mrs Goldsworthy had become General Wachtendonck's mistress, and the general, when not in bed with this good lady, was busily conspiring with her husband and the masters of British ships in the port. Such was the tenor of a dispatch[103] from General Maillebois to Mirepoix in April 1740.

It was shortly before that date that we have a fleeting glimpse of Theodore. His incarceration in the citadel of Gaeta had not been unpleasant; indeed according to a contemporary account,[104] he was "treated in a most genteel manner", which included permission to have his portrait painted (see illustration facing p. 85). Tactfully "released" early in 1739, he claimed later that he had sailed,

incognito, on a *felucca* from Terracina to Corsica, where
he spent two days in conclave with the Regents. After that,
he vanishes. To Rome? It is possible, even probable. His
good friend Sister Angelica was there (she died in 1740);
and it is conceivable that he may have cadged some money
either from his old employer, Cardinal Alberoni, or from
the Jacobite clique round James Stuart and his young son.
After all, he had served the Stuart cause in the past, and a
little loan from one "King over the water" to another might
be offered and accepted without offence—might it not?
Ripperdà was dead, over a year ago, and the Boon syndi-
cate in Amsterdam was done with him. Apart from the
Fonseca sisters, Alberoni and the Jacobites were the only
obvious "touches" for Theodore in Italy—unless, indeed,
he got some money from Don Carlos or his minister,
Montalegro.

There is no certainty here; but money, during that obscure
year, he somehow raised. For on February 7, 1740, he
suddenly appears in Cologne. Arriving in a post-chaise,
with three companions in Prussian dress, he called first on
his relative, the Grand Commander, then rented a lodging
in the city. Furnished apparently with ample funds, and
seen abroad with a childhood friend, Baron von Slein, he
wrote many letters and discussed with a local tailor a
contract (never completed) for the manufacture of a
thousand military uniforms. Three weeks later, he left
Cologne in a hired carriage, with a single servant. Giving
it out that his destination was Danzig, where he would
charter a ship for Corsica, he passed through Hanover—
and vanished again.

Where he went, and how he lived, is anybody's guess. In
the archives of the Quai D'Orsay there are letters which
passed, in the autumn of 1740, between Theodore and his
step-brother-in-law, M Gomé-Delagrange, of Metz, who

had married a daughter of M Marneau. The king wanted
to know what the French really meant to do in Corsica.
Delagrange replied that it was "not his affair". Undeterred
by this rebuff, Theodore returned to the attack. "My role is
not finished," he wrote; "I am in a position to make good
all lost ground." He went on to praise the Corsican exploits
("*une action sérieuse*") of Rauschenburg in 1739. and mentioned that he had great hopes of the Freiherr's younger
brother. Less praise could be accorded to "Colonel"
Friedrich, whose actions in '38 (after his betrayal by the
writer!) had been *lâches*; and he (Theodore) had been the
victim of undeserved treachery and enmity. Seven times he
had barely escaped assassination at the hands of Genoese
agents—once in Venice (perhaps he went there, that year,
from Cologne), and once, in July 1740, in Holstein, where
the authorities (in tribute—shall we say?—to the memory of
Baron Görtz) had meted out to the miscreants "death by
the rope".

Despite persecution, slander and murderous attempts on
his life, the king—so he wrote to his friends—was confident
of ultimate triumph. After all, did he not have a just claim
to Corsican allegiance? While in Aleria he had excavated
the grave, complete with the family's armorial bearings, of
a Neuhoff who had been Viceroy of southern Corsica in
930. Surely if Delagrange would put all this (including,
one assumes, the magnificent lie about the grave!) to
Louis XV, French support for the restoration of a rightful
king would be forthcoming. Delagrange, nonplussed and
reluctant to be compromised in this ploy, sent the correspondence to Amelot, who seems to have shown it to
Cardinal Fleury and then marked it, marginally, "no
action".

After that correspondence—from an address (as always)
undisclosed on the writing-paper—the curtain of the dark

falls again: Theodore goes underground, in a Europe about to explode in war for the Emperor's throne. On October 20, 1740, Charles VI took sick and died. Philip V of Spain at once made a bid for Austria's Italian provinces, while a Prussian Army advanced into Silesia against Maria Theresa, and Charles-Emmanuel of Savoy threw in his lot with Maria Theresa and her husband, Grand Duke Francis, against the menace of Philip and Don Carlos of Naples.

In that confused, insensate clash of arms, the King of Corsica, his claims overshadowed by the vaulting pretensions of greater rulers, lay low. Various scraps of news about his doings occasionally crept into the pages of the Press. Theodore had been seen in Venice, in Copenhagen; there is better evidence that, for a time, he was living in Siena.[105] Exactitude is not very material. Substantially, from his disappearance in late February 1740, until his reincarnation, under English auspices, over two years later, Theodore's history is that of a hunted adventurer with no fixed abode and no visible means of support.

Picture him thus in Tuscany, in Naples, in the Republic of the Doges. The scarlet caftan had long since been discarded, with the Moorish slippers and the swaggering Cavalier hat which had decked the pantomime king. His vanity now had to feed on the flattery of hangers-on and rogues, of whom Bigou, Duffour and Gio Ludovici were not the worst. Money—or rather its lack—was a persistent curse: pretending to have the secrets of Don Carlos to sell in Florence, and the plans of Grand Duke Francis to market in Naples, he was back, in regal guise, at the business of "free-lance agent". But it was a precarious life, made possible only by an occasional gift from Baron Drost: Theodore's journeyings left behind, then, a trail of unpaid bills, cheated inn-keepers.

"Why not try England?" This casual question by Bigou
set Theodore thinking. He still enjoyed—did he not?—the
panache of royalty; and the English, he had learned from
previous visits, loved a king. So to England, once more, he
went, in the early months of 1732. Still able—for all those
tell-tale bags of skin below the eyes—to exercise the old
douceur, he succeeded somehow in "selling" important
persons—including Lord Carteret—with the merits of his
cause. According to Horace Walpole, whose correspondence with Horace Mann, the British resident in Florence,
gives us a colourful picture of this phase of Theodore's
career, he won the heart, or at least the interest, of Lady
Lucy Stanhope, who interceded with Newcastle on his
behalf. However that may be, the curious fact—omitted
discreetly from English school text-books—is that in
November 1742, H.M.S. *Revenger* (Captain Barkley) sailed
from England to reinforce the English squadron, now
commanded vigorously by red-faced, short-tempered
Admiral Matthews, in the Mediterranean. On board,
treated as V.I.P., was the exiled King of Corsica. For
what purpose? To serve what "perfidious" British aim?
The French, to say nothing of the Spaniards, were soon
to ask that question insistently.

According to a report published by the *Mercure de
Hollande* in its issue for January 1743, *Revenger* put in at
Lisbon, having lost her main top-mast in a storm. Securing
a top-mast from "another vessel", she sailed without delay.
"Theodore is on board with £100,000 . . . on his way to
Corsica, whose crown he will offer to the Infant Don
Philip, becoming his Viceroy. It is understood that this
plan has been concerted with the Court of St James's—
from which the inference is that peace between Britain and
Spain is at hand." (In its next issue the *Mercure* averred,
more guardedly, that Theodore's support came, not

governmentally from the "nation of shopkeepers", but from "a powerful English trading company".)

Having next called at Villefranche, *Revenger* arrived on January 7, 1743, at Leghorn. There she was boarded by General Breitwitz, commanding the Austrian troops in Tuscany, and by Mr Goldsworthy, the British consul, whose failure to inform his superior officer, the Resident, about this conference[106] was judged by Mann to be "quite impertinent". In a letter to Horace Walpole on January 29, Mann wrote:

> Everybody's curiosity is carried to the highest degree, and all arts put in practice to discover who a great person is who is supposed to be on board a man-of-war at Leghorn, which furnishes great speculation for the Politicians there. Four persons are named for the stranger—the King of Sardinia, King Theodore, Admiral Matthews and, who do you think also? Why, Sir Robert Walpole! And do you know that many for a while seemed persuaded of it? The second, how-ever, is generally believed to be the person. His Corsican subjects at Leghorn make no secret of owning that they have expected him above a month, and among our folks at Leg-horn, the secret, I believe, has been ill kept, though most religiously from me. . . . 'Tis undoubtedly his Corsican Majesty, whose affairs, I greatly fear, may suffer from being discovered. . . .

"Discovery", of course, was inevitable; but that alone was not the cause of the luckless outcome of Theodore's final venture, under the English flag.

On January 18 a frigate (fifty guns) sailed from Leghorn for Corsica with the king's secretary, who was landed on the coast at Monticello, near Ile Rousse, with letters for the chiefs. On the outbreak of the European wars which fol-lowed the death of Charles VI, Maillebois and his French force had been withdrawn from Corsica. A new Genoese

governor, Domenico Spinola, had tried to revive[107] the
due seini hearth-tax, and there was new unrest in the island.
Theodore wrote that he would arrive in Corsica on January
26, and would proclaim an amnesty for all past offences
against his crown.

Some Corsicans appearing on the beach, an English
officer from the frigate went ashore (he spoke only Latin
beside his own tongue) and asked if the king would be
"received". The leader of the Corsicans replied cautiously
that there would have to be an Assembly. On that, the
officer decided to stay on the island pending the king's
arrival. He had to wait for some time. On January 28 the
Genoese consul at Leghorn, Signor Ravi, sent a fast *felucca*
across to Bastia with the tidings that Corsicans could be
seen embarking on the British warship, and that guns,
unloaded long ago from the *Yong-Rombout*, were also being
carried on board. During the night of January 29–30
Revenger slipped out of the harbour, accompanied by
Salisbury (fifty guns).

On February 1 the two ships were off Monticello. Two
more English officers went ashore to join their comrade
and invite such chiefs as had gathered to come aboard
Revenger and pay homage to their sovereign. A few accepted
the invitation, but Theodore did not land. He sent ashore
copies of a proclamation[108] which had been drafted in
Leghorn. An amnesty would be extended to all Corsicans
except (*a*) the assassins of Fabiani; (*b*) the "traitors" Paoli,
Arrighi, Salvini and Orticoni, who were condemned to
banishment, with confiscation of all their goods. All
Corsicans in Italy serving Don Carlos and the cause of
Spain must return forthwith to the island (this was presumably an English stipulation); but those in the employ
of Grand Duke Francis of Tuscany should continue
faithfully to serve him.

This proclamation distributed, Theodore decided (or, more probably, agreed with Captain Barkley) that the best plan for the moment would be to make a reconnaissance, by sea, along the coast. *Revenger* and *Salisbury* had now been joined by *Folkestone* (Captain Balchin), and to that ship Theodore was transferred. After an apparently aimless (or at least fruitless) cruise, *Folkestone* returned with the king to the coast of the Balagne on February 10.

Theodore's next move was to send a message to Captain Bertelli, in command of the Genoese garrison in the fort at Ile Rousse: if he wanted to avoid an assault, with no quarter, Bertelli must evacuate the fort at once, and send two hostages to the king. Bertelli complied (the British ships' guns were possibly a determining factor), and Theodore, taking courage from this *coup*, boasted that he could take Calvi without firing a shot. He did nothing to make good his boast; and, on February 12, *Folkestone* sailed back with him to Leghorn, where he approached General Breitwitz with an urgent request for troops to make good a landing.

Breitwitz, hesitant to take any action which might embroil his men in Corsica, referred the request to Vienna, and *Folkestone* rejoined her consorts off the island. The squadron then sailed south, and on February 28 was off Ajaccio, in whose harbour lay a damaged Spanish ship, the *St Isidore* (commander, Señor de Lage). A pinnace from *Folkestone* landed Theodore's secretary, who conferred for some time with the Genoese Governor. After his return, the English squadron[109] closed on the *St Isidore*, whose commander, rather than have his ship captured, set fire to the magazine. In the *sauve qui peut* thirty of his men were drowned.

Still the king did not land. Reports had reached *Folkestone* that the Corsicans, most of whom now pinned their hopes on eventual aid from Spain, had no more use

for Theodore; and the raid on the *St Isidore*, whose sur-
vivors were refused succour by the Genoese in Ajaccio,
doubtless made a bad impression. On March 14 *Folkestone*
landed Theodore, not on the Corsican coast but at the
mouth of the Arno, in Tuscany. The adventurer had lost
his "touch" at the game; the play-actor had grown rusty
in his regal "lines". The English king's ships had carried
him as passenger; his "cause", sponsored for a whim by
Lucy Stanhope, had served as an excuse for a naval raid on
the Corsican coast. But that was all. Theodore's sea-going
adventure with "perfidious Albion" was over: he never
smelt the *maquis*-laden scent of Corsica again.

CHAPTER THIRTEEN

Du Côté de chez Mann

THE "special operations" exploit of the English squadron
which destroyed the *St Isidore* in the neutral harbour of
Ajaccio may not have seriously displeased My Lords of the
Admiralty in London, but they were taken seriously
amiss in Genoa and Paris. While the Genoese Envoy in
Turin was voicing the Republic's complaints to Charles-
Emmanuel's minister, the Marquis d'Ormea—upbraiding
Turin for the crimes of her English ally in no uncertain
terms—Gastaldi, the ambassador of Genoa in London, was
protesting[110] loudly to high heaven and the Duke of
Newcastle. The poker-faced Secretary of State replied that
the action had been taken "without orders and contrary to
the policy of H.M. George II"; an inquiry would be held
and the Republic duly informed of the result. It never was.

The French naturally suspected the worst. Robert
Walpole (now Lord Orford) had fallen from office a year
before; and, under Pelham, the conduct of England's
foreign policy was now partly in Newcastle's, and partly
in Carteret's hasty hands. Amelot in Paris foresaw uncom-
fortably the trend of coming events. Fleury had died in
January 1743; with the Cardinal and Walpole no longer
working as a force for peace, a Hanoverian army, under

George II, was to come into conflict with the French forces at Dettingen that summer, nearly a year before the two countries were at open war. Amelot was accordingly eager to learn from his agents in the Mediterranean what devilry the English were hatching there in conspiracy with Neuhoff. Inevitably, poor Horace Mann, the British Resident in Florence, played in French (and Genoese) eyes the role of chief villain. Yet, though it is difficult to believe that the English naval operations could have taken place without the knowledge and tacit approval (blind eye, if you like) of Admiral Matthews—even if they had no official blessing from the Admiralty—Mann seems to have been, in fact, mildly revolted by English methods of semi-piratical warfare.

In February 1743 he had sent[111] to Horace Walpole a copy of Theodore's draft edict to the people of Corsica, and had received the reply that his friend wished Neuhoff success with all his soul. "I hate the Genoese," wrote Walpole; "they make a commonwealth the most devilish of all tyrannies." But it was all very well for Horace Walpole, in the elegant and cynical security of eighteenth-century aristocratic London, to criticize the lack of democracy in Genoese Government; it was quite another matter for Mann to cope, in Florence, with a complicated Corsican insurrection, on whose claims to English support he had no proper briefing. We find him, on March 19, 1743, writing to Walpole that "the *Mystery*" (Neuhoff) had come to Florence, and that he had had long talks with it, after dark.

> It has talked to me of its adventures, and strange they are. Lord Carteret is his great friend, but Lord Orford [Robert Walpole], he says, was the most attached to him. . . . I am at a loss how to behave, as I have no orders. . . . The affair seems to have been mishandled by the underlings of the fleet,

if it be true that the King, Lord Carteret and the Duke of
Newcastle gave such positive orders about it. . . . Meanwhile
King Theodore is upon our hands, and we are equally
embroiled, as there is nothing can be kept secret. . . .

PS. Jesus! A fourth letter from Theodore. He makes me
quite wild, as I cannot make anything out of his matters . . .
he is visionary to the last degree. I want to get him away, as I
think he is in infinite danger. I am to see him again after
dark, with a cloak and dark lantern. I am not used to it, and
by no means approve of it.

Here, surely, is the letter of a puzzled, unhappy diplomat.
Kept in the dark about the orders (if any) given to
Revenger and her consorts, he was "made wild" by Theodore without any certainty that the King of Corsica had
not got the unofficial backing of some members at least of
the English Government—as indeed, I think, he probably
had. A week later he wrote again to Walpole:

King Theodore is still here, but I have left off seeing him
as I don't hear or approve of the thing. . . . I confess to you
I should be glad of his success, but then I am too delicate to
wish England accessory to it. It will be no honour or credit,
nay, I believe quite the reverse. He told me an odd thing
which would justify the great intimacy he pretends to have
with Lord Carteret. He says Lord Carteret told him that
Lady Walpole applied to one of Hanover about the King to
induce the King to pity her. . . . The circumstantial manner
in which he speaks would almost persuade me that some part
is true.

An odd letter. It was common gossip that Lady Wal-
pole was the desperately unhappy mistress of Richecourt,
Vice-President of the Regency Council of Tuscany: Horace
Mann would know all about that. But how did Theodore
know, unless he really had been in "inner circles" in
London? The inference is strong that Carteret had, in fact,

been intimate with the exiled king, and had given him—together with much gossip of the town—his blessing for "unofficial" naval operations in support of Theodore's last, futile effort to get back to Corsica.

Mann, however, was still officially in the dark; he had written urgently to London for guidance and got no reply. On April 14, Horatio Walpole wrote to his worried friend.

> I have read your letters about *Mystery* to Sir Robert [Lord Orford]. He denies absolutely having ever had transactions with King Theodore, and is amazed Lord Carteret can; which he can't help thinking he must, by the intelligence [i.e. Theodore's intimate knowledge] about Lady Walpole. . . . You are quite in the right not to have engaged with King Theodore. Your character is not *Furibondo*. Sir Robert entirely disapproves of all *Mysterious* dealings; he thinks *Furibondo* most bad and most improper, and always did.

Let us accept Lord Orford's denials; he was no longer at the helm. Horace Walpole conceded that Carteret was probably "in it"; and he evidently took the view that *Furibondo* (Admiral Matthews) had improperly had a part in the "transactions" concerning King Theodore. How far the admiral had been a fully briefed executant of English policy is nevertheless doubtful, if we are to believe Mann. He wrote in reply to Walpole:

> *Il Furibondo* . . . is not more instructed from home than I am, or less embroiled. Such unheard of things are daily done by the fleet that do great discredit to England, and would make you wild . . . I have King Theodore still to deal with and to comfort in his disappointment. He writes me volumes every hour in the day, and most unluckily in such a character that there is no such thing as deciphering his letters, or even knowing what to say to him. Lord Carteret and the Duke of Newcastle have never answered me about him.

Poor Mann! He was suffering, as many diplomats did in the war of 1939–45, from lack of knowledge of "special operations" activities! His only consolation was a letter from Walpole, written on May 4, sympathizing with his troubles in having Theodore "on your hands". Characteristically, Walpole added the cynical quip: "He quite mistakes his province: an adventurer should come hither [to England]; this is the soil for mobs and patriots."

Reviewing the evidence more objectively, though with no love at all for England, Lorenzi, the French colleague of Horace Mann in Florence, was writing[112] to Amelot in Paris that it was "certain" that London had supported Theodore, but that the English had been "disillusioned" by their discovery of the hollowness of the king's boast that he had "12 munition ships and 100 trained officers" waiting in Italy for an expedition to Corsica!

English disillusionment or no, Mann had much still to put up with from Theodore. On April 18, 1743, the king left Florence (where indeed, as Mann suspected, he was probably in real peril from assassins in Genoese pay) and went to Pisa. From there he wrote to Captain Balchin of H.M.S. *Folkestone*, asking if he could be given a passage to England. The reply in effect was "Yes; but no royal honours, this time." Affronted, Neuhoff decided to stay in Italy. Taking cover—the Genoese Envoy at Florence was busily hiring assassins—in the house of Father Baldanzi, at Cigoli, near Florence, he kept up a flow of letters to Carteret and Admiral Matthews, pleading for either English naval support or—less majestically—transport by sea from Leg' horn to England. Matthews (who had now received orders[113] from London not to become "further engaged") left Theodore's letters unanswered. Lord Carteret's silence, too, was absolute. By the autumn of 1743 the unhappy king, abandoned by the powerful friends he thought he had made in London, was reduced to an extreme of financial difficulty. Having been forced at Cigoli to sell his under, clothes for bread, he betook himself wretchedly—without money or companions—to Leghorn.

What did accompany him was his pen and ink—those tireless adjuncts to his adventures. Correspondence from the king (much of it intercepted by French or Genoese agents) flowed out of his humble lodging. To Father Colonna, in Corsica, he wrote,[114] in the increasingly querulous tone which was now becoming habitual to him, that "infidelity" in the island was a grievous trial. "I have suffered, and I suffer particularly for you people. All can be set right; but the inconstancy of subjects paralyzes me."

Theodore was tempted to make contact, that autumn, with the Jacobites in Rome. The preliminary moves for the "Forty-five" were already beginning. Stung by Dettingen, Amelot had sent to England an agent who returned with (highly exaggerated) accounts of the Stuart party's vitality. After Amelot's fall, assurances of French support were given by the "forward-looking" new Foreign Minister, Cardinal de Tencin, to James Edward in November 1743, and a French expeditionary force under Marshal Maurice de Saxe began to assemble at Dunkirk. Characteristically, in his uneasy sojourn in Florence, pestering Horace Mann, Neuhoff wondered if he could not extract something to his own advantage from that great ploy. His old employer, Cardinal Alberoni, was still in Rome (he died in 1752); and though Alberoni had with, drawn from the politics of this world into contemplation of the pleasures of the next, he might agree to commend his one-time agent's services once more to the Pretender.

There was, however, Theodore decided, one compelling reason against his linking his fortunes again with the Stuart cause at this stage. He could not do so without abandoning completely the hopes he still pinned on England and England's allies, Charles-Emmanuel III, King of Sardinia, and Maria Theresa's husband, Francis of Lorraine, Grand Duke of Tuscany. If we accept—and it is convincing—the account[115] of the usually well-informed French Envoy to Tuscany, Lorenzi, it was to Charles-Emmanuel that Neuhoff was now looking.

In April 1744—by which time Charles Edward Stuart, in Paris, had had to digest the bad news of the abandonment of Saxe's projected expedition—King Theodore, under the name of Baron von Bergheim, was occupying a little house on the outskirts of Siena. He was keeping in touch with Mann by letter; and, according to Lorenzi, had received 1,000 *zecchini* (about £450) from "English sources". With these funds, which came, in fact, from the British consul at Leghorn, he was reported to be mobilizing and training several Corsican "companies".

That this private army (if it existed, as a "force", outside Theodore's lively imagination) was recruited on any considerable scale is highly dubious: one could not raise much of an army with £450, even in those days. He could, however, pay a few mercenaries, in contrast to his recent destitution at Leghorn; and he had collected a handful of Corsican refugees as a make-believe "Legion", for which the Tuscan authorities, with casual charity, provided some arms.

From this base he opened a diplomatic campaign in Turin. He had a friend, Baron de Salis, at Charles-Emmanuel's Court, and he wrote again and again to the baron asking him to convey messages to the Piedmontese Minister, the Marquis d'Ormea. In these letters[116] he complains that English "silence" is inexplicable. (He had been bombarding Carteret as well as Mann with his petitions.) Why is England "hesitating"? At Siena he can already dispose of 6,000 to 7,000 Corsican volunteers. Could d'Ormea not be asked to persuade Admiral Matthews to transport this force from Leghorn to Corsica— letting the admiral know that the expedition would have the approval of Charles-Emmanuel? Lorenzi apparently believed that this "approval" was a fact. But de Salis seems to have made little headway with d'Ormea (perhaps he did not greatly exert himself); for, in May, Theodore was addressing his letters direct to the marquis.

It was with regret, he wrote, that he had to observe that he had not yet received instructions where his "Legion" should concentrate: it was now 7,000–8,000 strong. If His Majesty Charles-Emmanuel would only persuade Matthews to send three or four frigates to Leghorn, an excellent plan of operations could be carried out. First, Spezia should be seized by a landing from the sea; afterwards it could be garrisoned by a small English force as a useful base. The frigates should secure St Florent, at the base of Cap Corse, as a bridge-head. That done, "all the Corsicans in Italy, headed by their King, will land[117] and chase the Genoese out of Corsica". Meanwhile to assist the process of mobiliza-tion at Siena, it would be helpful if a "small advance" (it might have been hungry poet addressing rich publisher!) could be sent to "Van Haagan", care of Horace Mann, in Florence.

No reply seems to have been sent; but Theodore was undeterred. On June 5 he wrote to d'Ormea that he had dispatched his secretary to Venice with a message to the Corsican "Colonel" Count Marc-Antonio Giappiconi, now in the service of the Doges. Giappiconi was to com-mand the "Legion", and meanwhile would proceed to Turin "for instructions". It would be a gracious act if Charles-Emmanuel could bestow on this distinguished soldier the rank (and presumably the Piedmontese pay) of major-general. History does not relate whether Giappiconi ever went to Turin, or got any position in the army of Piedmont. He certainly did not command any forces on Theodore's behalf; not did d'Ormea answer any of Theodore's letters. For, though Theodore did not know this, the English and their Piedmontese friends had decided[118] that there were other fish to fry.

With Charles Edward busily conspiring in Paris, and war declared in May 1744 between England and France, Newcastle and Carteret were quite inclined to make a diversionary effort (if it could be done cheaply) to wrest Corsica, and its useful harbours, from Genoa's weak hands, and utilize the island as a naval base against the French in the northern Mediterranean. But they evidently had become—as Lorenzi had reported—"disillusioned" about Theodore. Instructions were sent to Mann to get in touch with a likelier patriot leader.

One may suppose that the Resident in Florence disliked his instructions; he was a humane and civilized person. But he carried them out. Having made contact with Domenico Rivarola, Mann sent this (now elderly) Corsican agent to Turin at the end of June 1744. There Rivarola was given the title of colonel, with an expense allowance of 3,720 *livres* a year and a salary promised of 1,284 *livres* when he should have raised two battalions of Corsican volunteers.

For a considerable time Theodore had no inkling of Rivarola's activities, or of the fact that the "sympathetic" Mann had double-crossed him. That autumn, from his quarters in Siena, he circulated in Tuscany copies of a manifesto[119] from the people of Corsica (dated from Corte, but concocted, one fears, in Siena) proclaiming the islanders' loyalty to their exiled king.

By the end of the year his funds, again running low, had

to be replenished by the Grand Commander. Accompanied by Count Poggi (who had been with him when
he had gone to Leghorn in the autumn of '36, and was still
"loyal"), a secretary, a chamberlain, two valets and a cook
—poverty for the king, when he had found a credulous lender,
was still a relative term—he left Siena and went into seclu-
sion in a small house near Volterra. There he got news that
the rebels in Corsica had renewed their activity. They had
captured the fort of San Pellegrino (against which poor
Costa had been unable to bring up his guns) and, according to the *Mercure de Hollande* (March 1745), they displayed
their indomitable temper by cutting off the head of one
Barigel and sending it in a bag to Governor Mari as a
present.

Armies marched and counter-marched across Europe;
not till the guns had thundered at Fontenoy in May 1745
did Theodore realize what was afoot in Turin. He was hurt
in his vanity, and angered (lately he had suffered from gout);
he wrote[120] to the Marquis d'Ormea as an injured man.
Rivarola was a treacherous type; to support him would be
to damage the interests both of Corsica and her rightful
king. Why had the marquis not answered any of the letters
sent him last year? He (Theodore) would gladly come to
Turin—travelling incognito as Baron von Haagen—if
d'Ormea so pleased.

To the marquis, Theodore's proposal was (it must be
presumed) a matter of indifference: he had died a fortnight
after Fontenoy. His successor, the Marquis di Gorzegno,
sought advice from the Resident at Florence. Mann's reply
was discouraging. Theodore, he wrote, was a "dangerous
man, without solid foundations". Gorzegno took the hint:
Theodore's letter was "filed for reference".

Unanswered, the king was growing desperately im-
patient. Charles Edward had landed in Scotland: would

this mean that Hanoverian England would now think better of aiding another pretender to regain a lost throne?

Among the records of the Quai d'Orsay there is a copy of a curious (intercepted) letter written on September 9, 1744, by Theodore to Messrs "Salwey" of Leadenhall Street. Why this complete silence from England? Lord Carteret, wrote Theodore, should be informed that, with a little naval help, he (Theodore) could land in Corsica at the head of 10,000–12,000 men. (The "Legion" was growing in strength!) He had sent letters to the Duke of Newcastle and Lord Harrington (William Stanhope, now Secretary of State for the Northern Department), as well as to Mann; but all had gone unanswered. As for himself, recent experiences had been disagreeable. In the last eighteen months he had been three times in prison. (There is no evidence to support this pathetic story; nor does it square with the proclaimed existence, round his quarters, of the famous "Legion".) In May his life had been in peril from four assassins whom he had disarmed and chased through the window—an affray whose consequence was that he was still afflicted with "a slight trembling of the hand". The signature is "von Haagen", the romantic imagination that of von Neuhoff.

Shortly after writing this letter, Theodore left Siena, passed through Florence, where he had a (probably embarrassing) interview with Mann, and arrived at Leghorn. This move, coupled with the fact that the king's host at Leghorn was an English merchant, who put at his disposal a little house on the outskirts of the town, aroused dark suspicions again in the mind of the watchful Lorenzi. His reports to de Tencin in Paris were first that Theodore was due to sail for Corsica, unaccompanied, but that he was procrastinating through "nervousness"; then, that a British frigate was on the way to convey him to the island; finally that Mann, tackled about this "plot", denied all knowledge of it, though it was still "almost certainly" true.

Lorenzi's—and de Tencin's—suspicions were naturally deepened when Charles-Emmanuel, on October 2—a fortnight after Charles Edward had entered Edinburgh—published Letters Patent under which the King of Sardinia, Maria-Theresa and George II jointly took Corsica "under their protection" in order to free the people of the island "from a tyrannous yoke". Shortly before this,[121] the Corsicans had elected Gaffori, the Abbé Venturini and Francesco di Matra (Xaviero's son) as their own "Protectors".

Alas for Theodore—the protective umbrella of the powers was not being opened for his benefit. That summer two Corsicans—Francesco Sarri, of Bastia, and Angelo de Bonis, a doctor—had arrived[122] at Turin to urge an early expedition in support of the Resistance. Villettes, the English Envoy, concurred; it remained only to make certain of the approval of the Grand Duke Francis. That obtained (it was implied in the Letters Patent of October 2), a signal was sent to Admiral Matthews instructing him to co-operate. Mann, one concludes, must have had an interview with Theodore—unless, perhaps, he simply bought him off with a propitiatory draft on the consulate at Leghorn; for, on October 26, he wrote to Gorzegno that he "had prevented the embarrassment of Theodore's going to Corsica". In view of the circumstances, "embarrassment" was not an over-estimate.

Early in November an English squadron, commanded by Captain George Townsend, appeared at Cagliari, in Sardinia, and there picked up Rivarola. On November 17, having landed Rivarola somewhere in the Balagne, Townsend approached Bastia and demanded the surrender of the town. Mari, the Governor, replied by firing on the ships; and a bombardment of Bastia followed, causing much destruction. Rivarola, according to the plan, was to have launched a simultaneous assault by land; but on November 18, as there was no sign on shore of the insurgents, Townsend broke off the engagement and headed for the mainland. On November 21 the squadron was in Leghorn, landing casualties and making good its damage. Townsend was in a bad temper. He wrote[123] at length to Villettes that he had been "dallied with", and that he had been unable to secure from Rivarola and the other Corsicans "anything of their plans". The squadron had "done all it could", wrote Mann to Gorzegno; but "without Corsican co-operation nothing could be effected". Theodore could have told him that much!

The Resident was perhaps less than fair to Rivarola. Strict time-keeping was not (nor is it today) a notable feature of Corsican character; and Rivarola, from Town-send's standpoint, was doubtless late in keeping his rendez-vous at Bastia. But on November 20 he appeared at the gates, with 1,400 men. Mari, rather than risk his life in the defence of his bombarded (and probably demoralized) town, got on board a *felucca* with his private, very consider-able, fortune, and made for Genoa; the garrison, 500 strong, surrendered.

French fears that England would now be able to obtain Corsica as a naval base were redoubled; but, once again, the Corsicans were their own worst enemies. Rivarola's success at Bastia was followed by a fresh outbreak of the feuds which had defeated Theodore. Gaffori and Francesco di Matra promptly complained to Turin that Charles-Emmanuel had backed "the wrong man"; Ornano, now inclined to collaborate with Genoa, did all he could to frustrate Rivarola; the ultra-nationalists were indignant, as they had been in 1736, that the island should be made a pawn in the policies of the Powers.

On March 5 Admiral Medley, the successor of Matthews, writing "from *Russell*, off of Mahon", observed[124] to Mann: "The affairs of Corsica appear in the greatest confusion by the dissentions and discords amongst the chiefs and the Corsicans." The worthy admiral was surprised that "the Austrians had expected any good of the enterprise". He added—as many sailors did, before and since—that it was "a little unkind to throw it all on the Fleet". In short, the promising start at Bastia led nowhere; a plan to capture Ajaccio came to nothing; the Corsican insurrection of 1745 flickered out in clan dissensions, like Prince Charlie's affair in Scotland. The English quickly saw that "Operation Townsend" was aborted. According to Césare-Rocca (*op. cit.*) Newcastle—set on an accommodation with Spain—had always been half-hearted about supporting Rivarola. In any event, Mann soon gathered that London had called off the affair. Shortly afterwards, the Genoese, reinforced, recaptured Bastia and took many prisoners,[125] Gaffori and Rivarola escaping.

There follows, so far as Theodore is concerned, an unhappy chapter of his stay in Italy. He was now indeed become a pebble washed up on a lonely beach by the great tides of the wars of the Austrian Succession and the Highland rising. Early in 1746—Charles Edward in retreat now from the Lowlands towards his last, fatal "field" at Culloden—Theodore was in Leghorn. In his cups he would say to his companions that he regretted, in 1746, not having abandoned those ungrateful Corsicans, in order to rejoin instead, the Jacobite cause against an England which had double-crossed him so perfidiously: he would have had nothing to lose in following Charles Edward to Scotland, and he might have acquired honour for the "name" of Neuhoff—to which (as we shall see later) he professed so much attachment. But it was too late now.

According to French and Genoese spies—and we may
well believe them—he was still talking of a return to Corsica,
some time in 1746. But who was to back him? On how
much fidelity in the island could he now count? He had
scarcely one friend left in Corsica, and England had written
off, not merely Theodore, but Corsica itself. According to
Caird (*op. cit.*) the unhappy partisans made repeated appeals
for help to Lord Bristol, now British Envoy at Turin. But
there was no response. In June 1746—while Butcher Cumberland, victor of Culloden, was trampling on a country
which his boots defiled—Mann was writing to Gorzegno
confirming, with polite (and hypocritical) regret, Villettes'
verbal message[126] that George II was now "disinterested"
in Corsica: naval forces were needed elsewhere, and it
was "hoped" (pregnant word) that Charles-Emmanuel,
dependent always on English money, would concur. He
did: foreign intervention in the cause of the Corsican
Resistance was over for a long time.

The confused European wars went on—Saxe, Conti,
Frederick of Prussia, Cumberland and Maria Theresa's
generals fighting their indecisive campaigns—but no
crumbs fell from that disorderly table into Theodore's lap.
In the autumn of 1746 he had still, when wine kindled
confidence, flashes of hope that Charles-Emmanuel might
help him; he asked Mann to procure for him a *laissez passer*
for Turin. Mann stalled on the request; but he had not
finished with his *Mystery*. In February 1747 he wrote that
Theodore was back in Florence, reduced to extreme
poverty, and, more than ever "boring" him. The king rarely
left the little inn where he lodged, and the *patrone*, his bill
unpaid, often refused his client a needed meal. In despair,
Theodore had pawned the Great Seal of Corsica; and—
Mann added ruefully—"he pesters me daily".

Lorenzi was still reporting to Paris[127] that there was a

possibility of a renewed Anglo-Austrian *coup* in Corsica; Maria Theresa, he heard, had promised Theodore aid, and a force was concentrating in Elba, under the command of "Colonel Mills", an English officer, who had been in Charles VI's service. But there was no truth in this story. From the patient Sister Francesca, Theodore raised enough money to redeem the Great Seal; but, politically, his bolt in Italy was shot. In August 1747 he left Florence, and the now hateful surveillance of the British Resident, for a little cottage near Pistoia. A month later he received from Grand Duke Francis, now elected Emperor, an order expelling him from Tuscany. For his journey home to Westphalia a small purse of gold accompanied the order.

The powers who had once played with the King of Corsica for their greedy purposes, or who—if you like—had been cajoled into supporting him by pausible promises which he could not fulfil, had nothing more then journey-money to offer Theodore. He was no longer of any use to anybody; and he was an embarrassment so long as he remained within reach of the still not wholly subdued Corsican rebels. So—away with him to Westphalia. Horace Mann, knighted for his elegant tenure of that cultured English outpost on the Arno, whither so many witty letters were delivered from Horace Walpole's cynical and salacious pen, was mightily relieved. He would no longer be "bored" by Theodore. The English have never had much affection for discarded puppets.

CHAPTER FOURTEEN

La Commedia è Finita

IN the fifteen months which elapsed between Theodore's explusion from Tuscany and his reappearance on a new, and unexpected stage, his movements are once more obscure. According to one (questionable) source,[128] he went first to The Hague, borrowed 1,000 ducats from Rademacker, the Prince of Orange's treasurer, and discussed with various merchants contracts for the purchase of munitions, including 6,000 military uniforms. The story is unlikely. Neuhoff's credit in Holland was surely exhausted: the consortium was vowing vengeance, and there was still the little matter of the "adjudicated" debts which he had sworn, in 1737, before the *Cour des Echevins*, to repay.

Altogether more plausible is the statement from the same source that the king endeavoured to play a backstairs part in the congress which met at Aix-la-Chapelle in March 1748, to settle the terms which ended the indecisive wars of the Austrian Succession. He might well have thought he could secure something—a small pension, say—as a casual trimming to the settlement between Charles-Emmanuel and Genoa, whose forces were still contending with a new rising, led again by Rivarola, in Corsica. After that, the only certain knowledge we have is that, during the summer of 1748, Theodore was staying with a relative in the country-side near Hamburg.

From there he wrote to Francesca Fonseca in Rome—a letter which contained at least one typically egregious falsehood. His correspondence, he said, was continually being intercepted, and he had no news of Corsica. Recently he had dispatched "an English ship" with munitions to Aleria (this was a bare-faced lie), but the Corsicans seemed to be "abandoned by God"; their inconstancy was earning them an odious fame. He agreed with Sister Francesca that it would be prudent to think no more of his Corsican kingdom; but "the honour of my name is at stake in sustaining the enterprise at the risk of my life".

Brave words from an adventurer now fifty-four years of age; but Theodore's pen, as we have seen, was always apt to run away with him. Had he now any genuine belief that he could return to Corsica after so many years? It is un-likely. He must have been aware that France, alarmed lest the King of Sardinia should seize Corsica, was sending to the island a strong preventive force under General de Cursay. But it is possible that, in his incorrigible vanity, he had not wholly abandoned hopes of English aid.

Indeed unless he cherished the illusion that his "powerful friends" in England might still do something for him, it is difficult to find a convincing explanation for his next move. Instead of retiring quietly in Westphalia, where he had kinsmen and friends to shelter him, he raised a "little loan"—it was to be the last—from the indulgent Grand Commander of the Teutonic Knights in Cologne. With that, he travelled to London, where he arrived in January 1749, and took rooms, as Baron Stein, in Mount Street, Grosvenor Square, near "The Mount" coffee-house.

From that reasonably elegant address he approached the

Dutch minister, Hop, who seems to have been willing—
out of pity or from sheer amusement—to launch the king in
London society. At any rate he took Theodore to a number
of distinguished receptions, and introduced him to the
circle of Lady Schaub, the wife of a wealthy Swiss, who
entertained on the grand scale. Gastaldi, the Genoese Envoy,
was outraged: vainly demanding that the Government
should expel Theodore from England, he reported ner-
vously to the Republic that, according to Lady Schaub, the
king was "waiting for a ship".

Gastaldi's alarm was groundless. In the witty, cynical
London society of the day, the presence of a king who had
lost his throne was a curiosity—amusing until one tired of
it. Nobody dreamed now of financing a crusade against
Genoese Corsica: but Lady Schaub had a show-piece for
her guests. On March 23, 1749, Horace Walpole was
writing to Mann in Florence that her ladyship had invited
him to drink coffee with the king. He had accepted because
he was "curious" to see Theodore, although generally he
"preferred oil paintings of famous men to the reality".

Writing, eight years later, in 1757, Walpole observed that
Neuhoff was, to his recollection, "a comely, middle-sized
man, very reserved and affecting much dignity, which he
acted in the lowest ebb of his fortunes and coupled with the
lowest shifts* of his dignity" (*Fugitive Pieces*). The play-actor
could still sustain a becoming role. At the time, Walpole
told Boswell that Theodore had been very silent at the
party; the other guests, Lord March and Sir Hanbury
Williams, had found him "stupid or proud", to which
Boswell replied, charitably, that he might be "so hurt with
his misfortunes that he was become sullen and indifferent".

---

* Walpole went on to narrate how some Englishmen had brought Theodore,
in Florence, a collection of alms. He pushed his bed aside and sat in a chair,
under the canopy, to receive the offering!

Let that pass. It is also arguable that if the king was poor
company, the reason was that he was now overcome, not
by the inconstancy of subjects, but by money worries. His
establishment in Mount Street was not cheap; debts to
tradesmen, flattered at first by "royal" custom, were
mounting up. A few months later, the French Envoy in
London, Levis-Mirepoix, was writing to Paris that, where-
as the present tenant of the rooms which the king had occupied on the eve of the expedition on *Revenger* was reaping a
rich harvest of entry-money by showing them to sight-
seers, Theodore himself was now bitterly poor. Catastrophe,
crowning and irremediable, came just before Christmas:
Theodore was arrested for a debt of £400, and lodged in
the King's Bench prison.

If we are to believe Gastaldi, the Genoese Envoy, he had
previously left his Mount Street rooms (now besieged by
tradesmen creditors) and taken sanctuary in an embassy.
From that refuge he was lured by a spy, who conveyed to
him a forged letter, ostensibly signed by Carteret, inviting the
king to an urgent conference. So Gastaldi—who adds that
the spy unwarrantably asked for a reward from Genoese
funds and was naturally refused. Whose spy then? Conceivably a creditor thought of such a stratagem: it is not
material. The hard fact, for poor Theodore, was that news
of his arrest brought swarms of other grasping creditors
with writs. Having no assets—unless you count the Great
Seal of Corsica—he owed at least £1,500. The problem
was insoluble; for no more help could be obtained
from Westphalia. The Grand Commander had "had
enough".

From Christmas 1749 until midsummer 1755, the King
of Corsica held his Court in the squalid misery of the
debtors' jail. Carteret and Lady Yarmouth are said
occasionally to have sent him a little money for petty

comforts. Horace Walpole once remarked[129] that he had a mind to commission Hogarth to paint his portrait. He had visitors, drawn to the prison by curiosity: they included Monnet, a French actor-manager of the day, and Dr Nugent, of the Literary Club. On some the king would bestow—for a modest fee—a knighthood in the famous Order of Liberation. "*Vesti la giubba!*" Think as harshly as you please of the rogue—it was the pitiable humiliation of a pantomime Lear; and Theodore had not the consolation of madness.

In his extreme of misery he thought endlessly of strata-gems whereby to secure freedom. The archives of the Quai d'Orsay include a curious letter, addressed from London, in July 1750, to Marshal Belleisle by one Gautier, a *provençal* living at No. 3, Tennis Court. The writer said that in the course of long conversations with the king, who had much correspondence from abroad, he had learned that a new rising was being planned in Corsica: the French in the island were in deadly peril of massacre—the "Sicilian Vespers" once again! Would the duke not consider lending Theodore £1,500? This sum, which would secure his freedom, could be loaned on the security of his "papers": from these, thus pledged, the full details of the Corsican conspiracy could be unravelled. The suggestion was in-genious; its author, without a doubt, was no other than Theodore himself. There was no such Corsican plot; and Belleisle naturally did not respond.

The months, the dreary years rolled on. For one moment, early in 1753, the prisoner had a tantalizing gleam of hope. On February 12 he was given an *exeat*, one day's leave of absence from confinement, "to transact his affairs". His business was an interview with Horace Walpole, who was engaged in planning an article which appeared, ten days later, over the signature "Fitz-Adam", in the columns[130] of the newly founded periodical, *The World*. Written in a characteristic medley of casual charity and cruel irony, the article was headed: DATE OBOLUM BELISARIO. After some preliminary reflections on the impermanence of earthly greatness—witness the fate of Dionysius of Sicily, Edward II, Richard II and Charles I—the writer came to the sad case of King Theodore:

> Surely Britain ought to shelter such Princes as have been victims for liberty—whenever so great a curiosity is seen as a Prince contending on the honest side. . . . Theodore, King by election . . . [enjoys] the only kind of title allowed in the excellent gothic constitutions, from whence we derive our own. . . . When he had discharged his duty to his subjects and himself, he chose this country for his retirement, not to indulge a voluptuous, inglorious ease, but to enjoy the participations of those blessings which he had so vainly endeavoured to fix on his Corsicans.

The constitutional, democratic monarchy of Georgian England thus indirectly flattered, "Fitz-Adam" touched on the matter of Theodore's creditors. Debts? Their existence on his "civil list" had to be admitted; but they had arisen

> . . . owing to no misapplication, no improvidence of his own, no corruption of his Ministers, no indulgence to favourites or mistresses. His diet was philosophic, his palace humble, his robes decent: Yet his butcher, his landlady and his taylor could not continue to supply an establishment which had no means to support it, no taxes to maintain it, no excises, no lotteries to provide funds for its deficiencies and emergencies.

Hope, however, was in sight. Mr Garrick, out of his kind-ness, would give Theodore a benefit-night (a performance of "the self-dethroned Lear" would be appropriate), and would

thus "rival Louis le Grand as the Protector of exiled kings".
Nay more: the King's Bench would become "as renowned
through Garrick's generosity as the Savoy had been for
Edward III's treatment* of King John of France". Finally,
Mr Robert Dodsley, the Pall Mall bookseller, had been
appointed "high Treasurer and Grand Librarian of the
island of Corsica for life", and would receive subscriptions from the public on Theodore's behalf at his place
of business. Admittedly, wrote Walpole, constitutional
Royalists might object that Theodore was a monarch by
election, not divine right; but this should be no obstacle
to sympathy. Indeed any who for that reason withheld their
subscriptions would be, in the writer's view, self-confessed
Jacobites!

Readers of *The World* seem to have taken all this for a
pure jest; in the next issue a note was inserted that the appeal
for public subscriptions was seriously intended. Mr
Dodsley, however, received only £50; and Theodore, stung
by this jocular Press treatment of his affairs, ill-advisedly
threatened the bookseller with a writ for libel. (Irritated
by this "ingratitude", Walpole wrote to Mann on April
27, 1753: "I have done with countenancing Kings.")
Garrick duly gave the promised benefit-night; but the
proceeds sufficed only to pay off less than one-third of
the creditors. Freedom, for Theodore, was as far off as
ever, and his health, in prison, was beginning to fail.
On May 12, 1754, he wrote[131] to the Dutch diplomat,
Count Bentinck:

Illustrissime Seigneur et Très Honoré Cousin.

Having recovered somewhat from my wretched sickness, I
venture to have recourse to your Excellency asking your good

* It was a bitter jest! King John died with suspicious suddenness in the Savoy
on the night of April 8–9, 1364.

offices in finding me the necessary assistance to secure my release from this terrible (*funeste*) imprisonment. My credit is all gone, and I have been obliged by my sickness to sell everything I had, so that I now find myself on the verge of starvation (*à la veille de crever de faim*). In this state of things I implore you to find for me the assistance of a loan of £1,000, with which I can settle everything here and set off for your part of the world. Have pity on my deplorable condition, for which I am not in the least responsible, recommending my case to your friends. I am still confined to my bed.

Two months later, he sent a second despairing letter, imploring aid in his "last state of wrechedness".

Through want of cash I do not know where to turn. . . . I ventured to write to the Duke of Portland, begging him to assist me; but I had the mortification to learn from my messenger that he was surprised to find that I should think of writing to him, as he knew nothing of me. Unless something is done, and you kindly intervene, I can only look forward to see myself perish, actually wanting the common necessaries. . . . Deign to send me an answer under cover to Mr Da Costa, in Devonshire Square.

It was not until May 1755 that Theodore was released from his long confinement. Three years earlier a parliamentary committee had investigated the conditions of those indefinitely imprisoned for debt (its members visited Theodore in his cell); and early in 1755 the royal assent was given to an Act (28 George II) for the Relief of Insolvent Debtors. Under its provisions, permissive powers were accorded to the King's Bench to release bankrupts who published a complete statement of their assets, to whose possession the creditors would have sole title. The document signed by Theodore at the Old Bailey on June 24

THEODORE'S HANDWRITING

Portions of letters written in 1756 to Count Bentinck

(MSS. British Museum)

described the signatory as "Theodore-Stephen de Neuhoff, a German from Westphalia, and late of Mount Street, Grosvenor Square".

No talk any longer here of kingship. Under the heading "Schedule of Effects", he declared: "That he is entitled to the Kingdom of Corsica, and hath no other estate or effects but in right of that Kingdom." It is to be feared that the unpaid creditors had scant comfort from this declaration, but it enabled Walpole to write later to Mann: "You may get it indicated to the Pretender . . . that he has nothing to do but to pay King Theodore's debts and he may have very good pretensions to Corsica."

Theodore was not the only victim of Walpole's salty wit.

On his release, the king seems to have felt that he owed Walpole something—despite the careless malice of the article in *The World.* He sent him the Great Seal of Corsica. Touched, it may be, or feeling a twinge of compunction, Walpole proceeded to insert in the *Public Advertiser* a fresh appeal on Theodore's behalf:

AN ADDRESS TO THE NOBILITY AND GENTRY
OF GREAT BRITAIN

On the behalf of Theodore, Baron de Neuhoff

The Baron, through a long imprisonment, being reduced to very great extremities, his case is earnestly recommended for a contribution to be raised to enable him to return to his own country, having obtained his liberty by the late Act of Parliament. In the late war in Italy the Baron gave manifest proofs of his affection for England; and as the motives of his coming here are so well known, it is hoped that all true friends of freedom will be excited to assist a brave though unfortunate man, who wishes to have an opportunity of testifying his gratitude to the British nation.

Contributions were to be sent to Sir Charles Asgill, Alderman & Co., bankers in Lombard Street; or to Messrs Campbell and Coutts, bankers in the Strand.

It may be that the "nobility and gentry" were not convinced about the sincerity of the baron's affection for England in the "late war". At all events, Theodore was not "enabled to return" to Westphalia. During that autumn he was seen wandering about London in rags; and, towards winter, returned for a time to the King's Bench prison. It is uncertain whether he was re-committed there at the instance of an unsatisfied creditor, or went back simply for shelter and a crust to eat, rather than wander the streets, homeless and without food. Early in December he emerged again. The sequel was narrated to Mann by Walpole: "He took a chair and went to the Portuguese Ministry, but did not find him at home. Not having sixpence to pay, he prevailed on the chairmen to carry him to a taylor he knew in Soho, whom he prevailed on to harbour him."

The tailor, whose name is not recorded, was a humble man, with all the kindness of the poor; he worked and dwelt at 5, Little Chapel Street. There Theodore took to his bed—for the last time. Next day he was desperately ill; racked with pain, he lay on a pallet in a bare room above the tailor's workshop, his dulled gaze turned to the decrepit ceiling. Did his fevered mind see in its cracks a fancied outline of a distant island whose scent had once filled his nostrils? Only his kindly host's mongrel dog was there to keep him company as chamberlain; but memories, we may imagine, came crowding in—the sunny March landing, twenty years ago; the cheers round the flower-strewn dais in the square at Alesani; the armada assembled so confidently by Lucas Boon; the English sailors on *Revenger*. Round the dying man there must have also been many, too many,

ghosts; Luccioni, riddled with bullets in the evening sun-
light; faithful little Costa, dead of a broken heart; the
Sarsfield girl left stranded in Madrid; and—from further
back—"Madame", Görtz, Alberoni and Ripperdà, all a
little contemptuous, surely, of their protégé's ill-success in
"seeing it through".

> *Qu'est-ce qu'ici qui vient si tard,*
> *Compagnons de la marjolaine?*

It was much too late now. Far away in Corsica the Resistance had once more taken up arms against the Genoese;
but the patriots' cheers, this time, were not for the "unani-
mously elected" king, but for Pasquale Paoli, the little boy
who had trotted behind his father Giacinto, in Theodore's
company at Venzolasca, two decades ago. It was written,
long since:

> ἦθος ἀνθρώπῳ δαίμων.

Men are betrayed by what is false within. Commanding
neither trust nor fear, redeeming vanity with neither loyalty
nor courage, a self-indulgent crook with vaulting ambitions, Theodore had been his own executioner.

For two days the king lay in the article of death: the little
tailor did what he could, and the dog was faithful; but the
candle was guttering. December 11 dawned bright and
windy. Through the attic skylight the breeze blew a yellow
leaf which fluttered down on the dingy pallet. To the
dying man it may have seemed that it had fallen as the
chestnut leaves fell on that wintry march from Sartène
across the Bavella forest to the sea.

He had worn motley then—his great scarlet cloak
against the cold. *Divestita la giubba*: it was cold in the tailor's
garret, but the motley was all doffed now, even the Great
Seal given away. Climbing the stairs towards midday, the

tailor found his royal guest, Baron Theodore Stephan von Neuhoff, *unanimo consensu Rex Corsicorum electus*, cold and stiff in death, his wide-open eyes staring at a little withered leaf. Beside the bed, the dog whined, raised his muzzle and howled.

EPILOGUE

"Cup Coronets Gilt"

THE President of the Immortals had done with the King of Corsica. Two years later, Voltaire was to have sport with his memory in *Candide*; and he figured ludicrously as the hero in one of Pasiello's comic operas. But, before that, he had exercised once more the nimble pen of Horace Walpole. "Your old royal guest", Walpole wrote to Mann on January 6, 1757, "is gone to the place which, it is said, levels kings and beggars; an unnecessary journey for him who had already fallen from one to the other." Walpole seems to have relished his quip; for the idea burgeoned in his mind.

To the tailor's home in Little Chapel Street there came, on the evening of Theodore's death, an oilman of Compton Street, Soho, by name Wright, and clearly well-to-do; he said that, for once in his life, he would like to have the honour of burying a king. The honour cost him £10 11s. 2d. For this sum, Mr Joseph Hubbard, undertaker at the Four Coffins and Crown, near Carnaby Market, provided a seemly funeral show, including "a large elm coffin, covered with superfine cloth, finished with double rows of brass nails, a large plate of inscription, two cup coronets gilt, and four pairs of Chinese contrast handles gilt, with coronets over ditto". The interment was in the paupers' corner of the graveyard of St Anne's, Soho. Walpole atoned for this (or so he thought) by causing an inscription (to which the churchwardens at first demurred) to be erected on the outside wall of the church:

NEAR THIS PLACE IS INTERRED
THEODORE, KING OF CORSICA
WHO DIED IN THIS PARISH, DECEMBER 11, 1756,
IMMEDIATELY AFTER LEAVING THE KING'S BENCH PRISON
BY THE BENEFIT OF THE ACT OF INSOLVENCY;
IN CONSEQUENCE OF WHICH HE REGISTERED
HIS KINGDOM OF CORSICA
FOR THE USE OF HIS CREDITORS.

The grave, great teacher, to a level brings
Heroes and beggars, galley-slaves and kings.
But THEODORE *his moral learn'd ere dead;*
Fate pour'd its lessons on his living head,
Bestow'd a kingdom, and deny'd him bread.

It is doubtful whether Baron von Neuhoff would have greatly appreciated Walpole's carefully polished epigram; but I think he would have approved the "cup coronets gilt" on the coffin. Corpses in Corsica fared less handsomely; the play-actor had an elegant epilogue—though maybe he told St Peter that the "cup coronets" were solid gold.

CHRONOLOGY

1694 August 24: Theodore Stephan von Neuhoff born.

1697 *Peace between France and the Grand Alliance signed at Ryswyk.*

1701 *Duc d'Anjou crowned as Philip V of Spain.*
"James III" recognized by Louis XIV.
Grand Alliance re-formed.

1702 *Accession of Queen Anne.*
War of the Spanish Succession begins.
Charles XII invades Poland.

1708 Theodore appointed page to Duchess of Orléans.
Jacobite expedition to Scotland fails.

1709 *Charles XII flies to Turkey after Poltawa.*

1711 *Dismissal of Marlborough.*
Theodore begins military career.

1713 *Peace Treaties of Utrecht.*
Theodore with Elector's army in Bavaria.

1714 *Accession of George I.*
Charles XII returns to Stralsund; Görtz becomes his Chief Minister.
Philip V marries Elizabeth Farnese; Alberoni all-powerful in Spain.

1715 Theodore, disgraced in Munich, returns to Paris.
Death of Louis XIV.
Jacobite rising in Scotland.
Theodore takes service under Görtz.

1716 Theodore visits England.
Gyllenborg Plot.
Anglo-Austrian alliance.
Law founds Bank in Paris.

1717 *Triple Alliance: England, Holland, France.*
Theodore goes to Madrid.

1717 *Alberoni invades Sardinia.*
1718 *Austria joins Triple Alliance.*
Alberoni invades Sicily; Byng destroys Spanish fleet off Cape Passaro.
Cellamare's Plot.
Theodore in France (?) and Sweden(?).
Death of Charles XII.
1719 Theodore in Madrid.
Execution of Görtz.
Jacobite expedition from Spain to Scotland.
Marriage of Theodore to Mary Sarsfield.
Alberoni falls, succeeded by Ripperdà.
Flight of Theodore to Paris.
1720 *Crash of John Law.*
Theodore leaves Paris for The Hague.
1721 *Treaty of Madrid, between France and Spain.*
Theodore in Holland as free-lance spy.
1722 *Walpole made First Lord.*
1724 Theodore in Italy under alias.
1725 Theodore in touch with Jacobites in Rome.
1726 *Fall of Ripperdà. Fleury First Minister of France.*
1727 Theodore in Paris, and in London.
1729 Rising in Corsica begins.
1730 Theodore in Italy.
1731 *Treaty in Vienna.*
1732 Austrians crush rising in Corsica: Theodore in prison at Leghorn.
1733 *War of Polish Succession begins.*
1734 Fresh rising in Corsica.
Theodore becomes agent for Corsicans.
1735 March: Theodore goes to Tunis.
October: *Don Carlos becomes King of Naples.*
1736 March: Theodore lands at Aleria.
April: Theodore crowned.
August: Defections of Corsican chiefs.
November: Theodore leaves Corsica.
1737 February: *Chauvelin falls, succeeded by Amelot.*
March: Theodore in Amsterdam, arrested for debt.
April: Theodore released.
June–September: Voyage of *Agatha.*

13

1737　October: Death of Francesco dell' Agata.

1738　February: French land at Bastia.

September: Theodore's Dutch armada off Corsica; Theodore goes to Naples, is imprisoned at Gaeta.

November: *Treaty of Vienna.*

1739　April: Rauschenburg lands in Corsica.

French crush Corsican rebels.

June: *Spain and Naples adhere to Treaty of Vienna.*

October: *War begins between England and Spain.*

1740　Theodore in Germany.

Charles VI dies; war of Austrian Succession begins.

1741　French forces leave Corsica; Theodore in Italy.

Fall of Walpole.

1742　Theodore in England.

1743　January: *Death of Fleury.*

February: Theodore off Corsica in H.M.S. *Revenger.*

June: *Battle of Dettingen.*

1744　Theodore at Siena, approaches Government of Charles Emmanuel.

War begins between Britain and France.

1745　May: *Battle of Fontenoy.*

July: *Jacobite rising in Scotland.*

November: British land Rivarola in Corsica.

1746　April: *Battle of Culloden.*

Theodore in Italy—his bolt shot.

1748　French occupy Corsica: Theodore in Holland.

Peace Treaties of Aix-la-Chappelle.

1749　Theodore emigré in England; arrested for debt.

1756　Death of Theodore.

NOTES ON SOURCES

[1] Rostini: *Mémoires*, reprinted by the Abbé Letteron, Bastia, 1882. Rostini, a Corsican who lived in Rome, visited Corsica in the winter of 1736–7. His account is politically partial, but interesting, on account of its date.

[2] Notably Gregorovius (*Wanderings in Corsica*, translated by T. Mino, Edinburgh, 1855), and Count Varnhagen von Ense (*Theodore I*, published in *Bulletins de la Société des Sciences Historiques*, Bastia, 1894).

[3] *London Daily Post*, April 20, 1736.

[4] *L'Histoire de l'Isle de Corse* (Nancy, 1749), signed G. de C., but attributable probably to François-Antoine Chevrier.

[5] See Appendix I for conflicting versions.

[6] Giovanni di San Fiorenzo: *Account of Baron Neuhoff*, 1736.

[7] ANON: *History of Theodore I*; J. Roberts, London, 1743. This pamphlet, incomplete in many details, is more accurate than some other contemporary accounts.

[8] San Fiorenzo: *op. cit.* According to *Das Alte und Neue Corsica* (ANON; published by Peter Conrad Monath, Nuremberg, 1736), the father's name was "Leopold". It is not very material.

[9] Quoted by P. Fitzgerald: *King Theodore*; London, 1890.

[10] San Fiorenzo: *op. cit.*

[11] "Colonel Frederic": *Mémoires pour servir à l'Histoire de la Corse*, 1768. Le Glay (*Theodore Neuhoff*; Monaco, 1907) showed conclusively that he was not Theodore's son but an adventurer (he was a Pole, by name Vigliawiski) who endeavoured to exploit the Theodore tradition after his "father's" death. Finally, at the end of his resources, he shot himself outside Parliament in London.

[12] Osini, in his preface to the bogus *Testament de Theodore I* (Montpellier, 1895), says that he was seventeen.

[13] In Appendix III is given the disentanglement of various, con-flicting versions.

[14] Jaussin: *Mémoires Historiques*; Lausanne, 1758.

[15] Chevrier: *op. cit.*

[16] Rostini: *op. cit.*

[17] ANON: *Histoire des Révolutions de l'Ile de Corse et de l'Elévation de Théodore I*; The Hague, *chez* Pierre Paupie, 1738.

[18] Gregorovius: *op. cit.*

[19] ANON: *General Account and Description of the Island of Corsica*; Addison's Head, London, 1739; a colourful, though historically undis-criminating, pamphlet.

[20] Rostini: *op. cit.*

[21] Rostini (*op. cit.*) accepts the truth of this high-level sponsoring. The present author doubts it.

[22] Chevrier: *op. cit.*

[23] Chevrier (*op. cit.*) describes it as an "*aristodemocracie*". He points out that real power was concentrated in the hands of the "*Primati*".

[24] Gregorovius: *op. cit.*

[25] After this we hear no more of Ceccaldi. Presumably he died; but no record can be found of his death.

[26] *Memoirs of the Duke of Ripperdà*; London, John Stagg and Daniel Browne, 1740.

[27] Rostini (*op. cit.*) was in Leghorn in 1737 and is known to have been acquainted with Canon Orticoni, who probably gave him this impression.

[28] Césare-Rocca: *Histoire de la Corse*, 1916.

[29] *General Account.* A dispatch, dated April 12, 1736, from Mr John Bagshaw, H.M. Consul at Genoa (*State Papers*, Record Office), contained the report that "there arrived in the Rhoade [roads] of Aleria the *Richard* Galley, Richard Ortega master. . . . This ship belongs to Mr Consul Lawrence of Tunis." On April 26, however, Consul Bagshaw forwarded to London a complaint from the Republic of Genoa which referred to the master as "Captain Dick, otherwise known as Ortega (? Diego), the natural son of Mr Lawrence".

[30] *Robinson Papers*, MSS., British Museum.

[31] Rostini: *op. cit.*

[32] A large portion was translated by Mr Best and published in the *English Historical Review*, April 1886. The account is valuable, the more so because the European Press, during 1736, published only scraps of news,

mostly "angled" by the Genoese, about Corsica. Remarkably, the *Mercure de France*, though it was full of the doings of "*le Chef*", seems to have been totally unware of his identity.

³³ San Fiorenzo: *op. cit.*

³⁴ Cambiagi: *Istoria di Corsica*, 1770. Cambiagi was inclined to rely on the Press reports of 1736–46; his evaluation of degrees of truth was indolent.

³⁵ Chevrier: *op. cit.*

³⁶ The text of this letter found its way into the columns of the *Mercure de Hollande*, May 1736.

³⁷ This letter, found by Le Glay (*op. cit.*) in the Genoa State Archives, was forwarded by Marneau to "M. le C…", with the remarks: "Although I know him to be a man of wit and intelligence, very attractive … I regard this king as an adventurer with nothing to lose and only his temerity to spur him on. … My family and I are not tempted to seek our fortunes round a throne so shaky." Marneau was a shrewd man.

³⁸ Gregorovius: *op. cit.*

³⁹ Letteron: *Correspondance des Agents de France*. Bulletins, Bastia, *op. cit.*

⁴⁰ *Robinson Papers*, MSS., British Museum.

⁴¹ Letteron: *Correspondance*.

⁴² Pommereuil: *Histoire de l'Ile de Corse*, 1779.

⁴³ A copy of the Genoese declaration and Theodore's reply was sent to London by Mr Consul Bagshaw (*State Papers*, Record Office).

⁴⁴ Chevrier: *op. cit.* This writer states that, during a visit to Corsica in 1740, he spoke to eye-witnesses of the incident. He adds that, during his visit, a French lady with whom Theodore "had relations", was still in Corsica. She was, it is to be inferred, the Mlle Champigny to whom Theodore (see p. 119) was writing in November 1737.

⁴⁵ According to Fitzgerald (*op. cit.*) a small factory was set up in Naples for the manufacture of "Theodore" coins. The tale is congruous with Neapolitan character, and the present-day sale of cameos.

⁴⁶ *General Account.*

⁴⁷ Letteron: *Correspondance*. The *Mercure de France* (August) had better information. It wrote of "growing dissensions" among the insurgents.

⁴⁸ Letteron: *op. cit.*

⁴⁹ Rostini: *op. cit.* The *Mercure de France* (August 1736) carried a different story. According to this version, an attempt to assassinate Theodore resulted accidentally in a shot hitting and killing Fabiani.

Rostini's account, however, is too circumstantial to be dismissed in favour of a Press tale.

[50] Cambiagi: *op. cit.*

[51] This Proclamation, dated June 16, 1736, nobly printed by Mr John Baskett, is in *Robinson Papers*, MSS., British Museum.

[52] *Saggio Storico di Corsica*; Venice, 1768. The *Mercure de Hollande* (August 1736) says the news of Dick's death by his own hand was brought to Marseilles by a French ship from the Levant.

[53] Varnhagen: *op. cit.*

[54] *Histoire des Révolutions*, 1738.

[55] *State Papers*, Record Office: dispatches from Mr Bagshaw.

[56] The composition of the party is variously described by French agents (Letteron: *Correspondance*) and others. The author has taken the lowest common denominator of probability.

[57] M. de Campredon to Maurepas in Paris (Letteron: *Correspondance*).

[58] Battistella: *Ritaglie Scampoli.*

[59] Letteron: *Correspondance.*

[60] *Mercure de Hollande*, January 1737.

[61] Letteron: *Correspondance.*

[62] This phase in Theodore's career is fully documented by the *Mercure de Hollande* and dispatches from Holland in the Archives of the Ministry of Foreign Affairs, Paris.

[63] *Account of Theodore's Discovery in Amsterdam*—a document in the State Archives of Turin, quoted by Le Glay, *op. cit.*

[64] "Operation Boon" is described in detail by M. de Campredon, the French agent at Leghorn, and by M. Pignon, in dispatches to Amelot published by Letteron, *Pièces et Documents*, Bastia, 1893.

[65] Dispatch from Holland, Archives of Quai d'Orsay.

[66] The diary was seen by Campredon and Pignon (*Pièces et Documents*).

[67] Varnhagen: *op. cit.*

[68] Letteron: *Correspondance.*

[69] Galletti: *Histoire de la Corse*, 1863.

[70] Pignon to Amelot (Letteron: *Pièces et Documents.*)

[71] Pignon to Amelot (Letteron: *Pièces et Documents.*)

[72] *Pièces et Documents*, *op. cit.*

[73] *Pièces et Documents*, *op. cit.*

[74] Jaussin: *op. cit.*

[75] Galletti: *op. cit.*

[76] *Saggio Storico.*

77 Letteron: *Pièces et Documents*.

78 *General Account*.

79 Letteron: *Pièces et Documents*.

80 Letteron: *Correspondance*.

81 Letteron: *Correspondance*.

82 *Mercure de Hollande*, June 1738. Also Battistella, *Ritagli e Scampoli*.

83 *State Papers*, Record Office.

84 Letteron: *Correspondance*.

85 *Mercure de Hollande*, January 1738.

86 In subsequent accounts (see Note 88) of this expedition, the ship is described alternately as the *Briderost* and the *Preterod*—both of which are incongruous names. In the author's opinion the name was almost certainly that of the famous Dutch castle, Brederode.

87 A copy, sent home by Mr Consul Goldsworthy of Leghorn, is included in *State Papers*, Record Office.

88 The sources for the whole of this saga are (*a*) François Vastel's statement to the French consul at Alicante on November 7, 1738; (*b*) the diary kept by Riesenberg; and (*c*) the report of M Villeheurnois, Commissaire at Bastia. All are included in Letteron's *Pièces et Documents*.

89 Letteron: *Pièces et Documents*, *op. cit.*

90 Jaussin: *op. cit.*

91 Dispatch from Mr Consul Goldsworthy, *State Papers*, Record Office.

92 The *Mercure de Hollande*, November 1738, reports that he had accepted a bribe from the Genoese, and tried to fire the ship. This is plausible. Other accounts of this tragic incident depict the victim as a "super-cargo" employed by the Dutch merchants and put to death by Theodore because he tried to stop chicanery with the cargo. These versions were probably Genoese propaganda.

93 Renucci: *Storia di Corsica*, 1833. Also Pommereuil: *op. cit.*

94 In its issue of March 1739, the *Mercure de Hollande* reported that Theodore had hung off Ajaccio "waiting vainly for a signal"; and that then the weather got bad and "blew the ships off the island". A kindly version, in which one detects, once again, the "public relations" skill of Mijnherr Boon.

95 Archives, Ministry of Foreign Affairs, Paris.

96 George Gordon: *The Annals of Europe*; London, 1740.

97 George Gordon: *The Annals of Europe*; London, 1740.

98 Letteron: *Pièces et Documents*.

[99] Letteron: *Pièces et Documents.*

[100] Letteron: *Pièces et Documents.*

[101] Letteron: *Pièces et Documents.*

[102] Caird: *History of Corsica.* Also in Gordon: *op. cit.*

[103] Archives of the French Ministry of Foreign Affairs, quoted by Le Glay: *op. cit.*

[104] Gordon: *op. cit.* Also Galletti: *op. cit.*

[105] This is supported by Battistella: *op. cit.*

[106] The *Gentleman's Magazine*, in March 1743, carried a story (of doubtful authenticity) that Theodore had reached a secret understanding with Maria Theresa and her husband, Duke Francis. In return for an annual subsidy of 500,000 florins, he would place Corsica "under the protection of Tuscany", which would have the right to maintain a garrison of 12,000 regular troops in the island.

[107] Caird: *op. cit.*

[108] Text published in *Mercure de Hollande*, March 1743.

[109] *Mercure de Hollande*, April 1743.

[110] The text of this Note was published in the *Mercure de Hollande*, April 1743.

[111] The Mann-Walpole correspondence, here quoted from, is drawn, in part, from Doran: *Mann and Manners at the Court of Florence*; and in part from *Letters of Horace Walpole*, edited by Lord Dover, London, 1883.

[112] Archives of the French Ministry of Foreign Affairs.

[113] *Mercure de Hollande*, dispatch from Tuscany, May 1743.

[114] Genoa State Archives, quoted by Le Glay: *op. cit.*

[115] Archives of the French Ministry of Foreign Affairs.

[116] Giuseppe Roberti: *Carlo Emmanuele III e Corsica.*

[117] It is perhaps worth recording that in March 1744 the *Mercure de Hollande* published a dispatch from Tuscany reporting that Theodore still had "adherents", and that his hopes had been revived by the fact that Genoa was now at loggerheads with Turin over Finale (ceded to Charles-Emmanuel as a bribe in the Treaty of Worms). The *Mercure* confirmed that Theodore was "making approaches to Turin".

[118] Roberti: *op. cit.*

[119] The *Mercure de Hollande* published the text of this manifesto without comment. Declaring that Theodore was the one legitimate King of Corsica, it announced that this declaration had the force of "*une loi pragmatique*". The phrase suggests Theodore's penmanship.

[120] Roberti: *op. cit.*

[121] Césare Rocca: *op. cit.*

[122] Roberti: *op. cit.*

[123] *Egerton Papers*, MSS., British Museum.

[124] *Egerton Papers*, MSS., British Museum.

[125] Caird: *op. cit.*

[126] Roberti: *op. cit.*

[127] Archives of the French Ministry of Foreign Affairs.

[128] *Anecdotes* of Monnet (a monk) in State Archives, Genoa.

[129] Fitzgerald: *op. cit.*

[130] Walpole reprinted the article in his *Fugitive Pieces*, Strawberry Hill, 1758.

[131] These letters, of which passages are reproduced, facing p. 172, as an illustration of the calligraphy which so puzzled Horace Mann, are in the *Bentinck Papers* (Egerton MSS., ff. 387 and 423) in the British Museum. There is no reason to suppose that Bentinck was, in fact, Theodore's cousin.

APPENDIX I

Horace Walpole, in *Fugitive Pieces*, writes of the birth of
Anton's son as "about 1696"; but there is, in fact, little doubt
that Theodore Stephan von Neuhoff was born, at Cologne, on
August 24, 1694. The *Mercure Historique et Politique de Hollande*
of April 1740 reprinted a statement to this effect which
Theodore had just published in Cologne. ("King Theodore
recently published his titles in Cologne, as follows: Theodore
Stephan Baron von Neuhoff, Freiherr of Pungelscheid, Rade,
Lybach, Meuchausen and Safferan; born Cologne, 24 August,
1694. . . . Has three cousins, sons of his father's brother; one
Johann-Friedrich von Neuhoff. . . .") Neuhoff was an inveter-
ate liar; but his scholarly biographer Le Glay (*Theodore Neuhoff*,
Monaco, 1907) points out reasonably that a man in the lime-
light would hardly publish a fictitious date for his birth in the
city where he claimed to have been born, and where his state-
ment could be readily checked. San Fiorenzo (*op. cit.*) says that
Theodore's mother was brought to bed while on a visit to a
"noble family" in Westphalia. Furthermore, writing in 1748 to
Sister Fonseca, a nun in Rome who had befriended him,
Neuhoff mentioned his birth date as being August 24, 1694.
He had no motive for lying to the *religieuse*.

Like Horace Walpole, the 1743 London pamphlet gives
1696 as the date of Theodore's birth. Varnhagen von Ense, a
diligent German writer of historical travelogues, who visited
Corsica a century ago and clearly studied this pamphlet, seems
to have carelessly transcribed "1696" as "1686". From that slip

of the pen much confusion was caused in the minds of later biographers. The author of one colourful life of Theodore proceeded to erect a dramatic scaffolding of events in which he might be supposed to have cut a figure, if he had been born in 1686. By 1708, readers were told, he had seen action as a soldier in Bavaria, and had entered Swedish service. After a year spent as confidential secretary to Baron Görtz in Gottorp, he accompanied Fabrice in 1710 on a mission to Charles XII, then exiled at Bender in Turkey. There, readers were asked to believe, he spent a year—rejoining Görtz in Vienna, early in 1711.

Romantic suppositions—though these are by no means the only fictional accretions to the Theodore myth. But alas! These adventures have to be discarded in our quest for the hard bones of fact. All possibility of Theodore's having made this Odyssey to Bender, or of his having had any connection with Görtz or Sweden in this decade, is excluded by the unimpeachable evidence that, in 1709, he was a page in the household of the Duchess of Orleans at Versailles. The present author has the support of CésareRocca (*Histoire de la Corse*, 1916) who accepts 1694 unequivocally as the date of Neuhoff's birth.

APPENDIX II

Mr Geo. Tilson to Mr Robinson.

Hanover, 10/21 June, 1736.

I received yesterday the favour of yours of the 13th instant, and put it into His Excellency's hand, with King Theodore's letter to his kinsman. As you think everything that tends to discover the life and actions of this Knight Errant is to be admitted, I send you enclosed what I met with in a Paris letter in our hands.

THE PARIS LETTER

. . . His father, still young, married a Bourgeoise of the little town of Visé [Viseu] near Liége. Quarrelling with his family

on this account, he went to France and managed to secure
(*parvint à avoir*) the command of a fort near Metz. His wife gave
birth there to two children—Theodore, and a girl married to
the Comte de Trévoux. The Comte de Mortagne, madly in
love (*éperdument amoureux*) with Madame Neuhoff, took charge
of her children. He put Theodore among the Pages of
"Madame" at Versailles. There Theodore showed himself
adept in learning all that becomes a man of quality. He was
good looking and well built, and had a noble air. He had
charm (*douceur*), rather than brilliance, but his charm hid an
inordinate vanity. That, and debauchery, were his besetting
sins.

Leaving the Pages, he had an offer from the Duke of Birrenfeld, of a Lieutenancy in the Regiment of Alsace, then stationed
in Strasbourg. But Theodore did not wish to leave Paris, where
he had *liaisons* which he could not hope to find in the Provinces.
The Marquis de Courcillon, whose *mignon* he was, then pro-
cured him a company in the cavalry regiment of which he was
Colonel, and being the son of the Marquis d'Angeau, could
get him leave frequently to enjoy (for several years) *libertinage* in
Paris. The Marquis having died, Theodore got into hopeless
debt, and was hauled up (*cité*) before the Marshals of France.
Unable to meet his debts, he left France and joined Baron
Görtz, whose secret agent he became. He was in Madrid when
Görtz was beheaded. Luckily he found favour with Cardinal
Alberoni, who gave him the rank of Colonel, and a salary of
600 *pistoles*. Those seeking an audience with the Cardinal used
to approach Theodore, who thus made a lot of money—
between 10,000 and 12,000 *pistoles*—and became vain and
arrogant. . . .

He was advised . . . to marry a Maid of Honour, a relative of
the Duke of Ormond. This he did, and soon regretted it. His
wife was disagreeable—*d'un humeur revêche*. So Theodore, taking
advantage of the absence of the Court at the Escorial, fled to
Cartagena with all his wife's jewellery and took ship for France.
He arrived in Paris when the "Mississippi" speculation was at

its height. Mr Law helped him to means to pay his creditors and make a brilliant fortune: he was Plutus in flesh and blood. . . . When the System collapsed, Theodore's sister Elizabeth did what she could to help him. The Comtesse—no more chaste than Theodore—had a lover, the Comte de la Marck, who had been Ambassador in Sweden. Jealous of the affection (*intimité*) between brother and sister, he suggested to Theodore's creditors that they should secure against him a "*lettre de cachet*". . . . Thereupon Theodore fled to England, where he had adven‑ tures; and then proceeded to Amsterdam, where he made money out of Portuguese Jews. After that . . . little is known of his movements. Now, on the slippery stage of Corsica, if he escapes the scaffold, he will be a great man.

(The "Letter from Paris", here translated freely from the French and slightly abbreviated, bears no signature, but is clearly the pro‑ duction of a secret agent in British pay. It is included among the Robinson Papers in the British Museum.)

APPENDIX III

As an illustration of the tangled path which any biographer of Neuhoff must tread—picking up and discarding clues like a detective in quest of "the body"—here, for the amusement of historically minded readers, are the various extant versions of Theodore's brief military career, with the relevant sources.

(1) He served as a lieutenant in the Régiment d'Alsace—a position which "Madame" secured for him.

The 1743 pamphlet.

(2) He served with the forces of the Elector of Bavaria. ("I recommended him to the Elector, who gave him the rank of Captain in a good company.")

Letter of the Duchess of Orleans,
October 20, 1720.

(3) He was offered a lieutenancy in the Régiment d'Alsace by the Duke of Birrenfeld.

Mr Tilson's "Letter from Paris", 1736.

(4) He served first with the Régiment de Navarre; then, until the Peace of Baden (1714), in the Régiment de Courcillon; then in the forces of the Elector.

Letter from Marneau to M. le Comte . . .
April 26, 1736.

Put these versions side by side: what emerges? Marneau, Theodore's step-father, almost certainly comes nearest the truth. The Duchess, in a letter which went on to complain indiscriminately of Neuhoff's later misbehaviour, was thinking and writing only of the part she had personally played in his advancement. Marneau, now an elderly man, confused "Alsace" with "Navarre"—an easy slip. The 1743 pamphlet and the Paris agent were both accurate—at different dates.

Publishers' Note

We record with regret the recent untimely death of the author. Mr Vallance's last illness having prevented him from seeing his book through the press, we ask the reader's indulgence should any errors of omission or commission have crept in for lack of his invaluable supervision, despite our best efforts to eliminate them.

Index

195

$(16/-) \dfrac{a/n}{5/-}$ BP